The Map

A Personal Guide to the Sexual Marketplace

SOCRATES

MANNING UP SMART

Please send all inquiries to: Manningupsmart@gmail.com

First printing, 2018

ISBN-13:
978-1725945425

ISBN-10:
1725945428

www.manningupsmart.com

Preface

As an architect, I orchestrate a cross-discipline team of design professionals to respond to the challenges presented in the natural, social and cultural environment to create machines for living; architecture. Here where financial budgets are always tight, the forces of nature are persistent, the social and cultural forces are deeply challenging and yet there is a very real need my clients want fulfilled. They rely on me to guide them, to safeguard their resources and to make sure that the solutions we propose today will be viable in the future.

My professional background has provided me with a unique perspective on today's dating environment, where the challenges and hazards faced are often very similar and hold many parallels to the world of architecture. You need to understand and know the environment and context for which you are designing, provide a sold foundation upon which to build, and devise a structure to resist all of nature's loads. You must create an envelope with which to ward off the elements and put systems in place to make it habitable.

I help people understand and navigate today's sexual marketplace. I do this by leveraging the same approach I use in architecture; combining anthropology, biology, history, sociology and psychology to create a structural framework for living. This, coupled with my professional experience, allows me to create the vision and plan they need to achieve their life and relationship goals.

Many of my critics cannot talk honestly about what I will present in this book, because they haven't been able to enact it in their own lives or have no desire to... for any number of reasons; appropriately or otherwise. People unwilling or unprepared and frightened by todays dating and relationship environment will likely fail or avoid the ideas and concepts of *The Map*. Particularly if they listen to the howls of the naysayers. I should know, I too was very concerned about today's social, political and sexual environment.

Ultimately, if you want different results, you need to think, prepare and act differently. You don't have to become a statistic or be overcome by them. It is important to register this: when you listen to someone's life perspective and actively work to enact it in your own life you increase the likelihood that you will achieve similar results.

This book is the culmination of more than a decade of my personal experiences, academic and professional training, and my work with others in their self-improvement journey. It provides a working model to help you and others understand the framework, nature and references of today's sexual/dating market environment.

The Map aims to assist you with obtaining your relationship goals. This means understanding how and why several intermixed, complex and competing disciplines interact, how they will likely affect you, and how to respond when they do.

Have you ever asked;

Why do women prefer "bad boys" over "nice guys"?

What do women see in "those" guys?

Where have all the good guys gone?

Why is a condom your glass slipper in your Cinderella fairytale?

Why won't he commit?

What I am doing wrong?

Why can't I have the relationship I desire?

This book provides not only answers to these questions, but a framework for comprehension and a roadmap to follow for resolving those questions and more.

Never be lost in the Sexual Marketplace again!

To 'The Mary Frances': There were no short-cuts in finding you. You taught me that love is poetry lived and without you, I wouldn't have a future combined with yours, in the name of Elizabeth Grace.

If love is a battlefield, this book will teach you how to beat the yips, override your gut – and come home a winner.

If you watch pro baseball or play amateur golf, you know about the yips.

It could be you know *too much* about the yips: Every time you hear the term, you'll hear a slightly different explanation for the phenomenon. I can clear that clutter with two words: Spastic overcorrection.

The yips hit you when you are so obsessively concerned with not making a mistake that your obsession becomes its own meta-mistake.

You know all the right moves. You've studied all the right tips, tricks, tactics and techniques. You could write a checklist hundreds of items deep, of everything you must and must not do. Yet you become so overwhelmed by all that theory that – when it comes time to put it into practice – you crash and burn, often in humiliating, escalating and amplifying ways.

If love is a battlefield, the yips is shell shock, the fear that comes to be the greatest peril of all.

Here's the bad news: You can't get to second base if you can't get a second date. And you can't get a second date if you can't get a second chance. And you can't get a second chance if you can't even get to the second move in your game plan. You can only get shot down so many times before you start to feel like you'll never get up again.

Here's the good news: This book will help. Yes, it's more theory, but it's *better* theory, the theory that explains and corrects all the bad theory you've learned so far.

Here's the better news: Your problem is not a matter of tactics or techniques but simply the failure to understand the deeper biological and social motivations that are continuously driving you and everyone around you.

And here's the best news: Once you've learned to see what is *really* happening on the battlefield of love, you'll be that much better prepared to conquer it.

The bad news? You'll never be a 'natural,' the kind of guy who can make time with any woman, anywhere, anytime, in pursuit of any objective – or none at all.

How do I know that? Because that guy is not reading this book – or any book about navigating the sexual marketplace. What makes him so different? A lifetime of experience – with sisters and female cousins, most probably – that made him fearless around women before he knew he had any reason to be afraid.

You can't duplicate his experience. You can't relive your childhood. But you can learn the theory that he only understands vaguely, incompletely, mainly by habit and 'by gut.' And by mastering that theory, you'll know what he never learns: How to make love grow – and thrive enduringly – when it's more than just a matter of making time.

> "I've been thinking with my guts since I was fourteen years old, and frankly speaking, between you and me, I have come to the conclusion that my guts have shit for brains."
> —Nick Hornby, *High Fidelity*

I love that quotation. You may remember it from the movie – the only romantic comedy I can think of that actually 'gets' men – but that's the original form, from the book. It illuminates how the naturals, navigating the sexual marketplace by gut, are lost, too – just a little bit further on from where you keep getting stuck.

> "Human civilization is nothing but the answer to this one monumentally important question: How does a nice guy go about getting a second date around here?"

That quote's from me. It sounds like a joke, but it's not. Men made civilization to make sure that their offspring would not just survive but *thrive,* – proliferate enduringly in peace and prosperity. Not to make your case of the yips any worse, but this is not just a matter of getting the girl: You have the whole weight of the world on your shoulders.

Masculinity is leadership. Women nurture. Men cultivate. The forces of modernity work assiduously to undermine male leadership, but without a man in charge, nothing goes anywhere. That's easy enough to see; just look all around you.

But male leadership depends on romantic leadership – on getting to the altar, and from there to the nursery, by getting that second date. Shakespeare commanded that "The world must be peopled!," but you can't have grandkids if you don't have kids. And you can't have kids who can raise kids of their own kids if you don't have a wife. And you won't have a wife if you can't get beyond the yips, get beyond your gut, get beyond all the bad ideas that have been holding you back.

What's the cure for bad ideas? Better ideas. And that's what you'll find here – the better ideas about navigating the battlefield of love that no one has shared with you so far.

So here's the best news of all: You don't have to have the yips, and you don't have to have shit for brains. But you do have to have a plan, and that's what *The Map* gives you: A plan to make the most of your life as a man, a lover, a husband, a father – and as one of the irreplaceable cultivators of all of human civilization.

It's not easy bearing the weight of the world on your shoulders, but that's why men are so much stronger than women. But it's not enough to be strong, you've got to be smart, too, and that's what 'manning up smart' will do for you.

None of this is easy, but nothing worth doing is. But making your moves in that romantic battlefield just got a whole lot easier – now that you found *The Map-A Personal Guide to the Sexual Marketplace.*

"The mass of men lead lives of quiet desperation. What is called resignation is confirmed desperation."
Henry David Thoreau

Do not let the story of your life culminate in the story of unrealized dreams and potential. Act, engage, invest in your life and commit to action your potential, so that it may be realized and that you may drift into your grave having not just lived, but thrived.

To get the most out of this book, it needs to utilize it, not just read.

"Go West!"

Then share this book and ideas with a friend...

You can find more of my content at:

www.manningupsmart.com

YouTube: Manningupsmart

Or contact me at the following:

Manningupsmart@gmail.com

TABLE OF CONTENTS

AUTHOR'S INTRODUCTION

I've made mistakes. Though significant to me, in the grand scheme of human experience they are terribly common and banal.

I was ignorant. I had preconceived ideas and principles developed both on purpose and by default that I clung to no matter the circumstances - as if doing so would solve the issue at hand. I also closed my eyes to the context of the situation I was in. I didn't look objectively.

My biggest failure and the one that haunts me today are the failures of the self. Those times when I wasn't true to myself, my values and my belief in myself. I betrayed those who placed their trust, faith and love with me. Those personal failures played a direct role in the decisions I made that affected the quality and direction of my life. They also factored significantly in the relationships I sought out and developed.

To the people I hurt through my behavior I owe apologies I can never fully proffer. This book is in part my work in offering some of that apology; by knowing and doing better and by rectifying the errors of my ways and paying that debt forward to others so they are not tempted or make similar mistakes.

My failures cost me more than the relationships I soiled. They cost me the relationships I didn't have.

When you lose faith in yourself and stop acting upon and through your own values you can't possibly have anything but disastrous results. That's a given. Furthermore, doing so doesn't leave room for the relationships you genuinely want. The relationships you could have had with the people you were with and with people who you never knew - the ones who were wise enough to avoid you in the first place. The life you could have had gets lost because you are not the person you should have been. That cost is incalculable. It also rather disturbing to contemplate. It should be.

The MAP- A Personal Guide to the Sexual Marketplace

Ultimately this book is a reflection of some of the things I've learned and developed in reflection and study of my own life, from the individual I was to the person I've become. The biggest and most critical step in that journey was when I embraced a concept of agency; when I became a willing and knowing agent of my own life. Not a victim of circumstance. Not a bystander. Not looking for or giving excuses. But when I started to own my life, my past, my present, to help shape my future; to choose whom I wanted to be.

With that in mind I'm going to demand that you do the same. Before you do anything, you are going to need to own your own life and be responsible for it; to take time and reflect upon it and be honest with yourself.

I'm not here to give advice. I don't want to tell you what to do or how to do it. I don't want to be your parent. These are my opinions and I'm willing to share them. If you choose to take them, use them, they're yours to do as you feel and please, but you own them. You always own the opinions and advice you take. And when you do, they are yours. And so are the consequences of adopting them. That is the unspoken element associated with all advice. No difference here. I insist upon it. Your life is yours. It's not for me to tell you what to do. You should heed all the council you want, but be the captain of your own ship. Make your own decisions and be accountable for them.

I will also be upfront in stating I'm writing this book for a reason (beyond penance). I have a purpose in mind and it involves you. I'm here to champion a cause. I'm here to promote civilization, in whole and in part. As an architect, I plan and develop buildings that give rise and shape to our world. I design spaces for people, events, for business to flourish, prosper and to excel. My formal education focused on and highly promoted these notions and concepts; that design matters, that good design can and should change lives for the better. It can. Sometimes it does. More often it doesn't. It doesn't because it can't address the heart of the issue; that is we design for people, and when people are highly flawed, disadvantaged, and too misaligned to make proper use of a virtuous intent, that intent will fail. In short, I design hollowed, empty shells for people to interact with, in and around.

How do you best enrich civilization; by the environment in which people exist, or the people in their environment? Ideally, it's both, but only one directs the other. One leads the other and is a consequence of the former. People matter and people create societies, civilization and its resulting architecture. In that regard, architecture is a matter of ego, an expression of the self, an apparatus that reacts with the outside world and comprises a body and soul for its being. The problem we face is that the foundations of our society and civilization shows the signs of serious decay, instability and neglect in light of many of the changes we currently face today. This book is but one step to rectify that; to shore up our foundations as people, to start with individuals, to help shape partnerships, and to develop healthier families which have always been the bedrock upon which any civilization rests.

I also recognize that all movements are personal if they are to succeed. That means I need to develop an immediate connection to you directly and that my ideas resonate personally with you and in such a manner that you can see yourself in those ideas and be able to act upon them for the results you desire. That last part is critical. You need to be able to control, direct and decide the paths you take to the destination and objectives you desire, not just the ones I'm marketing or promoting, or anyone else for that matter. Yes, I'm here to promote committed relationships, but if that isn't your goal or objective that's fine. I can (and will) show you how to have the sexual life you want, stay single and maintain moral and ethical values in being honest and open about it. In doing so, you'll develop healthier relationships and interactions as a natural consequence and that is a better thing for society and civilization in general.

Each of us picking up and reading this book will be driven by any number of highly personal factors, but I want to direct the focus of this book toward a specific number of audience members. First, to those who don't understand the sexual marketplace (SMP) and feel lost and bewildered by it. Second, to those that are unsatisfied by their position in it and who seek to better their lives through understanding and corrective action. Those who do not want to rely on luck or serendipity for their happiness and fulfillment in the SMP and their established relationships; that is to say they are looking for explicitly repeatable elements, features and behaviors that will determine their relationship potential success, happiness and longevity. Oh, and it would bring me no small measure of joy if people found a degree of sheer elation in the titillating entertainment of the subject matter at hand, after having personally been put to sleep and mentally lobotomized by any number of scientific white papers discussing the same material. Sex should entertain as well as sell. I hope this book does both.

We will also need to recognize the limitations of this book and our discussion together; this book isn't a catch all. It will not solve your problems, though it may enlighten you and provide you with a tool for greater understanding and utilization for your life. It is a tool and reference only. You are your own solution. And as such, if you have the personality disposition that is self-defeating, promotes incompetence or is so religiously indoctrinated in your beliefs as to be hostile to opposing thoughts or ideas, please put down this book and ask for your money back. Immediately. Don't waste any more of your time and life by continuing. Really. Stop now. I have neither the time, energy nor the desire to help defeatist people who see problems in every opportunity or every difficulty as an insurmountable obstacle to their happiness and achievement. I also don't have time, energy or inclination for those waiting for the bus to arrive. It's not likely coming. You and I both know it. If you want to get to where you want to go, you're going to have to get up and start walking. I understand that the walking takes energy, that it might rain, that you'll surely suffer hardships along the way, as you leave the safety and security of your comfort zone, but this is where we part ways. Stay here, stay where you're comfortable. Wait for the world to revolve and the stars to align in your favor. You're fine the way you are. Things may change without your input, ownership or agency. Really, they might, there's no honest telling. I just believe it's unlikely.

I also find a tremendous measure of satisfaction and calmness in a degree of certainty and control of myself in my environment. I'd rather walk than wait, even if the resulting times for doing so were the same. Furthermore, if your life is tragic, I'm truly sorry for that. I wish it wasn't so. I really do. But honestly, I'm carrying my own load that I'm responsible for and I still have a long way to go. I can only take on so much more. I'm more than happy to share the road and our journey together, but I'm going to be on my way at this point. I hope you find everything in life that you want and that your life is a fulfilling one.

If you don't ask for your money back, I hope that you can embrace that with a measure of good will, as if you bought us a round of drinks at a pub and we were to then part ways. Thanks for the purchase. Have a nice life and good luck.

For the rest of you we're going to open a door and head through the threshold...

Sincerely,

~Soc!

CHAPTER 1
THE SEXUAL MARKETPLACE

'The Sexual Marketplace'... what a loaded term. It's loaded because it's laden with meaning that has significance, relevance and is full of unspoken import and connotations that reverberate with almost everyone. Most importantly it is EXACTLY what we are going to be talking about; sex, your sexuality, and how your offerings compare in an uncaring free market. It's a better term than anything else I could have used. I could have used the terms "relationship", "dating" or "marriage" environment, but I didn't because what we are going to be talking about covers far more territory than those. It is a far more inclusive term and I intend to talk about a far more expansive environment of human interpersonal interaction.

"Sex" as a term has its own highly electric energy, for good cause and reason beyond titillation. It's relevant because we'll be discussing elements of how people relate to each other sexually, so it's only fair that we speak clearly and honestly about the subject at hand. Why else do you think it was that Confucius said the beginning of wisdom, is to call things by their proper names?

'Marketplace' is another term that, in the context of sex, causes almost as strong a reaction from people as sex itself. We're ill-prepared or cultured to talk in polite company about terms associated with "sales", "marketing", "bartering", "trade" or "negotiations" as they pertain to sex. As you can guess, we're going to be talking about all those things in relation to you, your sexuality and the relationships you want or are in.

The worst part is that we're not going to ease into this; we're going to jumping right into the deep end of the swimming pool of human interactions. This is where the adults come to play. This isn't the kiddie pool or the shallow end where the seniors wade out and bob up and down in relative safety. Don't worry about being fancy or graceful about it. We're going to dive in with an inelegant splash, well, you are, I'm doing a cannonball right next to you. We're going to be swim buddies from this point forward; I'll teach you to swim and have fun in the deep end and you'll be my partner in making the world a better place.

Welcome to the deep end.

Take your last chance for a deep breath as you cling to the sides of the pool and savor our initial achievement. The achievement of honestly calling something by its proper name.

The Economic Model

For those of us in it, the Sexual Marketplace (SMP) is a screwed-up place. We intuitively feel what's going on but may not fully understand it. We're inundated with poor advice from those that are detached from reality, have social agendas, or who are just so clueless that it would be laughable if not for the very real damage they're creating. We are faced with poor advice, heady goals and the opposing stark realities in a very unforgiving dating environment. We reach out into this darkness and try to grope our way through it - too often with disastrous results. We don't understand it, have no way to interpret the conditions, our place within it, no chance to discuss it with others in meaningful ways, and have no confidence that we can repeat our successes.

The SMP is a nebulous environment in which a multitude of social, cultural, economic, political and biological drivers influence the underpinnings of human behavior. They are the same drivers that are shaping our society and in fact the SMP is a reflection and outcome of those. To understand the sexual marketplace we must realize that it is a reflection of those drivers, not independent of them.

Utilizing an economic model as an analogy helps us a great deal because it provides a framework for understanding, language we can use and comprehension of the forces at play and their inter-relationships between factors and drivers. For better or worse the 'sexual marketplace' is a marketplace like any other market, where the value of products and services being offered (you) are shaped by the forces of supply and demand, with governing agencies (cultural, social, political and biological) attempting to influence behaviors and outcomes found within it. And like any market, we can speak to macro conditions; the over-all scale or big picture elements that structure and shape the total sum of the market and micro conditions; the small, individual or personal level elements that drive supply and demand on an individual level.

At a macro level markets vary in form, scale, geographic and service niches. The SMP is no different. It can vary based on the form of the cultural, social and political environment in which you're operating. The scale ranges based on the number of active participants within that pool of people. Geography still plays a role, even though the SMP can take on a virtual form within the internet: on forums, chat rooms and dating sites, because people still want to connect in person and not just virtually. And while we may initially scoff at the notion of politics playing any role in our sexual lives, the realm of sexual politics is a very real and impacts your life whether directly or tangentially, as sex is highly political and promises to remain so in the future.

At a micro level the SMP varies based on the individual and reflects individual tastes, beliefs and values, both yours and your potential customers. All these elements shift and swirl around and what was true yesterday may not quite be true for you today, as preferences, beliefs and social sexual value adjusts over time. Time is an incredibly important component to the SMP as we'll discuss later when we discuss life trajectories and timeframes. Bottom line is that your individual mileage may vary when discussing the SMP; personal perspective, situation and context matters greatly.

With all that in mind it is important to point out that you are a business in this environment and together we are going to be looking at your potential customer base. In this regard, we will be shifting back and forth between you being both a product/commodity and a service provider offering a range of potential services to a willing and knowledgeable clientele. We will not be trying to sell our product and services to an unwitting customer base. If anything, we'll go out of our way to help educate our clientele prior to their decision and commitment with us. There will be no magical lines, silver bullets or seductive potions offered with short-term sales strategies. Doing so comes from a position of weakness because you know the quality of your offering is low and the client wouldn't purchase otherwise. We're better than that, we're thinking long-term and we're aiming to win the client again and again, building a loyal customer base in the process. Ultimately, they should see us as their valued option.

Not only are you a business offering a product and range of service, it means that you are also the CEO. Let that sink in for a moment. I'm not only going to expect you to manage the day-to-day operations of the business we call "you" but expect you to act and behave like an executive officer. You'll be expected to lead, look toward the future and plan appropriately in guiding your life and the relationships found within it. The sooner you learn, embrace and exemplify those qualities the better. As the CEO, you'll also be responsible for the team you build, and a cardinal rule of business is that the team you build is the company you build. We're not looking to be a massive growth, hire and fire type firm with a revolving door. We want to be one in which we steadily grow, with quality offerings, stability and an end-of-life retirement plan, because it comes not just from a promise, but from an ability to deliver.

Biological Drivers

You are the result of billions of years of evolutionary success, in massive part due to the fact that you're hard wired biologically for it. The great news is that on a biological level, we just have to get out of our own way, embrace our biological nature and let life happen. When we do, we will have fulfilled our part in keeping our species alive and project our unique genetic sequencing into the future. It is so simple a moron could do it. In fact, they do. In all actuality, individuals who have less mental capacity than a moron have been successfully able to complete this critical life circuit and our species has continued because of it. Yes, I'm looking at you Neanderthals.

We stand, evolutionarily speaking, not on the shoulders of giants, but individuals with remarkably small cranially capacities. I'm taking the point of view that doesn't look down our immediate family tree but along the depth of it: well past the human historical record, and into non-recorded history, beyond archaic humans and deeper into our humanoid past. Past Homo erectus, past Homo habilis, deeper than A. africanus and A. afarensis. For all these individuals' merits, to which we owe our existence, they had remarkably small brains but were genetically successful. They are what we'd call a Darwinian success as their children had children of their own. The reality is we don't need a large brain to survive, but we need to tap into and utilize the "primal" brain we're already sporting. Of course, if it was that easy, our discussion would be coming to a quick conclusion. I'd say go forth and behave in a primal fashion and all would be well in the world. We of course are not that simple, and it isn't quite that easy. Actually, we don't want it that simple. It is also a remarkably low bar to be setting, one in which I have full faith and confidence you are expecting to vastly vault beyond yourself.

Our primal brain consists of the upper root of the spinal cord and the basal ganglia known as the brain stem and parts of the mid-brain called the limbic system that supports a variety of functions associated with housing our emotional life and the formation and storage of our memories. These are the areas of the brain responsible for our early evolutionary success, in what Darwin was to describe as the basic mechanisms of evolution in Natural Selection. It is responsible for the functions associated with survival, provision and seduction. This primal brain developed much earlier (millions of years earlier) than our fore brains, which are responsible for rational and cognizant thought. It is important to recognize that the primal brain is not a center for learning or thinking; it is emotional in nature, it is also responsible for "all or nothing" type responses. It is reactionary by nature. The most common example is the survival mode within the limbic system associated with fight or flight. When you're in limbic/primal brain mode, there is no gray area; you're all in. It is either this or that. Furthermore, the limbic/primal brain actively shuts down your higher brain functions, the neocortex, those areas associated with reason and thinking. The limbic system doesn't want you to think, it wants you to act and act NOW, to the exclusion of everything and everyone else.

Our primal brain evolved to secure the first order for existence, that is to survive and then to reproduce. Our primal brain which serves as the foundation of all human behavior, our biological imperative, is guiding us to continually protect ourselves, provide for ourselves and then to procreate. As the foundation of human behavior, it also serves as a primary driver for the sexual marketplace. That is to say the primary basis of the human sexual marketplace is reactionary and is free of rational thought or thinking - which starts to explain a great number of things. That attraction and desire cannot be negotiated, and that attraction and desire are not a choice, but a biological reaction with absolute certainties in the decision making process (limbic decision making process). When we attempt to negotiate attraction and desire we are fighting nature and our base primal self and our base primal self-interest. When we condemn attraction and desire as a personal choice, we are ignoring the biological order of nature and ourselves. As such, we need to face the reality that attraction isn't a choice and attraction simply cannot be negotiated at a primal level.

The primal brain does more than create response reaction mechanism to compel us into action, it also is a signaling center to help promote decision making along certain lines by releasing chemicals and hormones in response to environmental stimulus or to aide in biomechanical requirements of the body. In part, it helps control effects on the body such as metabolism, immune system, circadian rhythms, growth stimulation, hunger cravings etc. This is all good stuff, but what we're really interested in are the parts that play an active role in our reproductive cycle, sex and memory response mechanisms that shape our decision making and the nature of the sexual marketplace.

It should come as no surprise that hormone signaling in puberty leads to the development of children into adolescents as well as the development of secondary sex traits such as beards and breasts. The importance of all this isn't just to note that the signaling occurs and their results, but that they are natural and primal functions. Puberty and adolescence is not only a physically transformational process, but one that has many psychological and emotional transformations as well, often the results of which dictate our sense of self, our perceptions of the world and what we can expect from it. Our real sense of our body image begins here. We become acutely aware of the changes taking place not only physically, but socially, as gender roles start taking a more pronounced tone and the structure of many of our relationships often change. The timing of these changes in relation to our peer groups also plays a significant factor, as early maturing boys are seen and received in a more positive way, whereas early-developing girls experience significantly more social problems associated with sexual activity, drinking, smoking, drug use, depression and eating disorders, as they struggle for a sense of self-identity and independence. At the end of the adolescent stage we will have either developed a positive and healthy sense of ourselves or will be confused, having misgivings and unresolved questions regarding our identity, role and place within the culture to which we are entering. It is at the end of adolescence that we fully enter into the sexual marketplace as adults and with it we are carrying all the emotional baggage from our childhood and pubescent years with us into it.

The MAP- A Personal Guide to the Sexual Marketplace

Likewise, genes and hormones actively influence the expression of many of our social behaviors, conduct and interactions with individuals, groups or within society as a whole and our reactions to them. This genetic inheritance serves as the innate qualities and social instincts for an individual. They also help formulate the critical elements of motivation and emotions central to human behaviors, such as fear, sadness, happiness, anger and disgust that promote and guide our basic behaviors. Hormones play a central role in our reward-based response system of motivation and memory formulation of those experiences too. Because sexual reproduction is essential to the survival of the species, genetic coding and hormonal motivation sequences play an enormous factor in human behaviors that give shape and context to the sexual marketplace. Mating preferences, reproduction strategies, parental investment and social constructs of cooperative behavior are but a few. On an individual level they influence our physiology for lust, attraction and attachment - all of which play enormous roles in our lives. When these hormones and neurotransmitters are triggered by the body we can interpret those sensations as love and formulate attachment bonds because of those feelings; even if the subject and nature of those bonds are unhealthy and a poor rational choice. Our primal brain circumvents the rational process to promote a short-term genetic objective. When we lose the capacity to control these impulses, we are subjects to the whim of biological compulsion.

We'd like to think that we're actually rational, thoughtful and introspective beings, when in reality we're in a constant state of being punch drunk. We are flooded with hormones and chemicals that are playing as behavioral influencer strings to our puppeteer genetics; a circumstance which essentially has not changed significantly for eons. Our motivations for behavior can be depicted by Maslow's model of the hierarchy of needs, and while simplistic in its schematic form and subject to current interpretations, it offers an immediate and valuable insight to some of the motivationally driven behaviors found with individuals and within relationships.

The MAP- A Personal Guide to the Sexual Marketplace

Maslow's Hierarchy of Needs Pyramid

The model is based on motivational theory; what drives people to do what they do and behave the way that they do. It focuses on a series of categorized levels of unequal weight and emphasis assigned to those needs, commonly graphically illustrated in the form of a pyramid. The creation of a motivator is initiated when there is dysfunction in achieving a particular need, which creates stress for the individual to resolve. The greater the stressor, the lower on the pyramid rung, and the greater pent up unfulfillment of that need, the greater the motivation and demand to satisfy that corresponding need. Hungry people desire food more than safety, frightened people look for safety prior to concerns governing love and belonging and friendships, lonely people will seek friendships and sexual intimacy before concerning themselves with values of esteem and respect, those that are lacking confidence, achievement and respect will not be concerned with morality or ethics. We also need to keep in mind that these needs are not static. They are all depreciable over time and once obtained need to be managed, maintained and sustained, and if eroded, repaired to maintain stability and satisfaction within each supporting category of human need.

For the most part when we talk about the Sexual Marketplace (SMP) we're talking about the middle three levels of the hierarchy of needs; Safety, Love/Belonging & Esteem, because that is where most of us currently exist. That makes up the largest part of the sexual marketplace. It is also where most of us have problems and issues because we are not fully aware, prepared or in a position to resolve those issues appropriately and move our connection with others beyond that.

Even at a basic level the sexual marketplace can be a very confusing and challenging environment to understand and comprehend, let alone express to others. Attempting to really delve into the subject departs wildly from what our purpose is, that of finding your results in the sexual marketplace of today: results in which you can command, sustain, maintain, that are of your choosing, and determined by you. In order to do this, it would be helpful if we had a set of tools that we could use to reference and to make sense of the sexual marketplace, to plan and realize our objectives accordingly and in a clear and concise manner. A map of the sexual marketplace would hold tremendous value in visualizing this complex environment, the major elements governing them and their interrelated relationships, all in easily understood format. This visual presentation of the sexual marketplace would help increases your understanding, comprehension and utilization of information far faster than if we just wrote or talked about it. To be really valuable, we would want the map to be simple enough for you to mentally recall it and have an intuitive feel for it, to be utilized on demand and on the fly if need be. Ideally, we would want the map to initially perform the following functions:

- Identify our place in the sexual marketplace. If we can't reasonably do this then for all intents and purposes we're lost. we just don't know where we stand or how we fare in the sexual marketplace, much less why.

- Determine what and where our objectives are. These are personally subjective, and we have full reign of the human dimension to choose from. Knowing where we want to go is central to getting there.
- Establish an appropriate action plan to get us to our objective. This is normally determined by connecting the two locations of where we are at and where we want to go together. This process not only creates a line, but the line denotes a value equation of what traits and values are attributable to getting there most effectively.
- The scale of the line, how large it is, will help us identify the scale of our undertaking in achieving our ambitions and is incredibly useful for preparation and planning purposes.
- It should also identify the skill level needed to achieve our goals, as our map should be able to identify value ranges between fundamental skills through advanced and refined skill levels. Knowing the intensity required of our ambitions is also a key influencer in preparation and planning to meet them.
- Lastly, we will want to know what obstacles will be present in our environment, when we will generally face them and then be beyond them, so you can plan and prepare in advance or by circumventing them altogether.

Our map therefore should reflect the graphical, scalable and measurable relationships between variable quantities of the sexual marketplace, so that we can appropriately plot and delineate between values within it. Now, what would THAT look like?

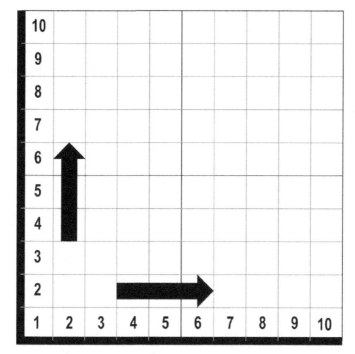

Prime Axes

Any graph is going to be comprised of two opposing sets of values set along their respective axis, in an X and Y fashion of a Cartesian plane. Our challenge is to identify what those two primary drivers of the sexual marketplace are. As primary drivers, I believe, they should be both basic (fundamental) and tremendously powerful (obvious) and I can think of no two single drivers more fundamental and obvious than biology and culture. The first governs our nature, what we are as a species, and the second is the single defining element that identifies who we are as a species. In regard to the sexual marketplace, we are going to be talking about selection, from what values, behaviors and beliefs people draw inferences and make decisions from and because of this we'll identify the X and Y axis of our graph as such - "Natural Selection" and "Social Selection" - and place them

The MAP- A Personal Guide to the Sexual Marketplace

on a scale from 1-10. The scale is rather arbitrary and we could use 10's, 100's or 1000's if we chose, but for simplicity's sake, we'll keep it pretty basic at 1-10.

Of the two principal factors governing the sexual marketplace, we are going to begin our discussion with the one that is unavoidable: natural selection. We are biological beings and while we can resist that, we are taking on a considerable task (nature & biology) in doing so. So, let's begin there.

10										
9	Hypergamy: a natural sexual attraction predilection of females for traits and behaviors associated in males with physical stature, health, fitness (**survival dimorphisms**), social standing, rank, displays of wealth, and resources (**provisional dimorphisms**) and displays of deliberate sexual enticement, provocation and execution (**seduction dimorphisms**).									
8										
7										
6	Hypogamy: a natural sexual attraction predilection of males for traits and behaviors associated in females with health, fitness and vigor (**survival dimorphisms**), youth, fertility and variety (**provisional dimorphisms**) and displays of deliberate sexual enticement, provocation and accessibility (**seduction dimorphisms**).									
5										
4										
3										
2	⟶									
1	2	3	4	5	6	7	8	9	10	

NATURAL SELECTION (Survival, Seduction & Provision)
PHYSICAL, SEXUAL & SOCIAL DISPLAY DIMORPHISMS

Natural Selection

Charles Darwin is synonymous with natural selection from his theory that originated in his seminal book *Origin of Species*. His insight and contribution to our understanding of evolution was to identify the mechanics that explained evolutionary change and an understanding and role of sexual selection in this process. He recognized that resources such as food, water, shelter and mate availability are limited, therefore individuals compete with each other to secure those scarce and essential resources. In addition, he recognized that if all individuals are unique, some will have variations that provide advantages to survival and opportunities to mate, transferring those traits to their offspring and over time, these traits will spread throughout the population, and consequently the population, as a group, would evolve; the corner stone of which is natural selection. Additionally, anthropologists, biologists, neuroscientists, psychologists and human behavioral researchers have all investigated physiological and psychological responses mechanisms and behavioral traits in humans associated with sex drive, attraction and attachment in pair bonding relationships. Furthermore there has been considerable investigation into intersex competition (within sex: male-male, female-female) and intrasex competition (between sexes: male-female and female-male) to curry attraction and attachment, all of which profoundly shapes the sexual marketplace.

Where, as humans, males and females faced similar challenges, we adapted similar responses to them, and therefore share similar selection traits of attraction. Both males and females will naturally select visually for and toward healthy, fit, and sexually mature individuals (survival dimorphisms) and those that further exhibit social traits, behaviors and courtship strategies associated with sexual display, deliberate enticement and communicating sexual receptivity (seduction dimorphisms). While the triggers are complex and selective to given individuals, it is to be noted that generally speaking the stimulus is proportional to the response; that is the greater the induced attraction stimulus, the greater the inclination and attraction response in return. If we're looking to evoke the "DAMN....!", response from potential mates, we need to be bringing the big 'D' and not the little 'd' in stimulus.

Inversely, where we differ is where, evolutionarily, we faced differing adversities that we were required to overcome through adaption, and therefore our attraction selection responses differ accordingly. Because of our shared mammalian lineage, females face a tremendous biological challenge of internal fertilization, which includes an elongated gestation period and nourishing their young in the form of lactation over an extended period of infant development. It would have benefitted females to sexually select a mate who could protect her and her child, possessed and commanded resources or the ability to acquire them, and a willingness to provide for her and her child, in addition to other social benefits acquired through this process (provisional dimorphisms). This inclination is called Hypergamy. Males on the other hand didn't face those adversities and therefore were better served with a mating strategy that increased the number (variety) of healthy and fertile females he successfully inseminated (provisional dimorphisms) and is referred to as Hypogamy.

Natural Selection:

	SURVIVAL	SEDUCTION	PROVISION
HYPERGAMY	*Physical Stature* Health Fitness	Sexual Enticement Sexual Provocation *Sexual Execution*	*Social Rank* *Wealth* *Power* *Fame*
HYPOGAMY	Physical Stature Health *Vigor*	Sexual Enticement Sexual Provocation *Sexual Accessibility*	*Youth* *Fertility* *Variety*

Hypergamy: a natural sexual attraction predilection of females for traits and behaviors associated in males with physical stature, health, fitness (**survival dimorphisms**), displays of deliberate sexual enticement, provocation and execution (**seduction dimorphisms**) and social standing, rank, displays of wealth, power and fame (**provisional dimorphisms**).

Hypogamy: a natural sexual attraction predilection of males for traits and behaviors associated in females with health, fitness and vigor (**survival dimorphisms**), displays of deliberate sexual enticement, provocation and accessibility (**seduction dimorphisms**) and youth, fertility and variety (**provisional dimorphisms**).

The MAP- A Personal Guide to the Sexual Marketplace

Our historical concepts for masculinity and femininity, confident and dominant projections are rooted here and individuals exhibiting or showcasing these traits tend to be referred to as being "alpha", as in the apex of dominant masculine or feminine expression of behavior and being. It is for this reason that these traits are often referred to as alpha traits.

The concepts governing hypergamy & hypogamy are thoroughly assimilated into mass culture (even if unidentified) and reinforced by various disciplines of scientific, anthropologic and sociological areas of research and study all too routinely to be anything but an un-egalitarian truth. What then does Natural Selection tell us about an unregulated sexual marketplace:

- As a species we are selective and will not mate with just any of our species (as opposed to fish for example) and as such, not all of us will either get an opportunity to acquire a mate or will be successful in doing so. There are going to be winners and losers in the game of life.
- The sexual marketplace is highly competitive amongst the sexes (male-male, female-female) and between the sexes (male-female, female-male) to acquire a mate, the successful typically employ mating strategies with an emphasis on aggression, dominance and threat of violence and that female competition is no less competitive than male.
- Nature tends to be violent, ruthless and conflict is a natural state of life. Taken to extremes, rape, murder and infanticide are viable mating strategies often found in nature.
- That we have a variety of strategic sexual pathways to find a mate; lust, attraction or attachment, individually, in combination or simultaneously and these factors don't have to be focused on a single individual but can be dispersed amongst several competing individuals.
- While we tend to be a monogamous species (we're mammals), the monogamous focus typically is only for a single breeding cycle

(4years), thus serial monogamy tends to be the predominant pattern naturally, which closely follows today's divorce cycles and our propensity toward remarriage.

- That mate poaching is a high effective form of mate acquisition and we have evolved biologically to support (promote) and to defend from such behaviors in our social environment.
- That genetic cuckoldry (paternal discrepancy) is still a considerable risk men face today.
- That both sexes are sexually disposable.
- That we should respond naturally to your sexual role.
- Nature doesn't have your long-term interests at stake; nature only wants you to be Darwinian successful; that is your children having children of their own.

If it isn't already apparent, this isn't a virtuous environment.

SOCIAL SELECTION
RELATIONSHIP, MANAGEMENT & MAINTENANCE SKILLS
(Team work, Stability & Intimacy)

	2	3	4	5	6	7	8	9	10
10									
9									
8		Social Selection: are those behavioral dynamics that relate							
7		to Team Building, Relationship Stability and Intimacy.							
		Team Building- Those skills that reduce tension, violence							
6		and anxiety; referred to as Relationship Skills							
		Relationship Stability- Those skills that serve to preserve a							
5		qualitative state; also known as management skills							
4		Intimacy- Those skills associated with affinity, rapport and							
		attachment; also known as maintenance and repair skills							
3									
2									
1	2	3	4	5	6	7	8	9	10

Social Selection

What stands in contrast to the natural environment and natural selection? Civilization. Society. Culture. They are the hallmarks of human achievement and are the most powerful and productive tools known to man. Culture, society and civilization stand directly opposed to and separate us from our base biological and animal instincts and it has taken us tens of thousands of years to get here. At its most basic, these social constructs of behavioral governance defuse social tensions, stabilize relationship structures and foster relationship bonding between parties and are the hallmarks of any civilization or society. These patterns of behavior are reflected and enforced in mating patterns in the form of social selections. Partnering provides tremendous advantages of specialization, support and task sharing, which culminates with the benefits of shared child rearing, a safer environment and the tremendous advantages gained for children raised in a stable, healthy, pair-bonded household, over children raised outside of such circumstances.

In our ancestral evolution from large troops of primates, which typically get upwards toward 50 individuals, we crossed a critical threshold where our tribes (social groupings) exceeded 150 or more. Researchers have noted that when social animals reach this level of group concentrations, they need greater and greater mental capacity to deal with the inherent social conditions present in these environments. While there is great strength and security in numbers, it also invites greater complexity as well, in having to deal with the internal social environment, which can become highly aggressive and lead to violence. To thrive in large social structures, we must have a good sense and understanding of the intentions and disposition of others, to be able to devise models of thinking and understanding, and to problem solve based upon these projections. An adaptation to these was a remarkable evolutionary shift from natural selection toward a self-feeding loop of social selection, where increased cognitive demands were met with increased refinement of social skills rooted in self-awareness, empathy, social cooperation and social skills; the center of which was language. Once these traits showed themselves for their utility, they became highly desirable traits sexually and a revolution in brain size growth development occurred. This is believed to have occurred due to the initial non-monogamous group structures associated with early hominids, where an individual gifted with these abilities could or would have been selected by a number of females to be impregnated by, thus the seed of his genius could spawn a generation of progeny with his potential. This theoretical situation has been actually observed and documented within chimpanzee societies where intelligent, creative and persevering individuals passed on more of their genes than did their lesser rivals.

I think it is terribly important to recognize that as a species we developed specifically to exist and to excel in large social groups and that our specific biological adaptations (large cerebral cortex) have helped us not only overcome challenges naturally found in our environment, but also further developed as a result of those complexities, challenges and risks found and emanating within large social structures as well. It is not in our human nature to succumb to environmental or social challenges, but to utilize our rational brains to formulate adaptations to address the challenges we face in any age. I refuse to believe that a species, that in less than 100 years discovered powered flight and repeatedly left the orbit of our planet to land on our moon, cannot or will not be able to address the social, cultural, political or legal challenges associated with life-long coupling relationships (marriage). Those challenges must and will be met individually because it is only on a personal level that your marriage matters to you. A million relationships can succeed or fail and the only relationship that matters to you is your own. Empowering the individual to take note, become versed in what those already known social adaptations are, and to gain sufficient experience and confidence in enacting them will be essential to this endeavor and your personal success and happiness.

Social Selections are those behavioral dynamics that foster and develop **Team Building**, models of behavior that promote **Relationship Stability** and interactions between individuals that promote **Intimacy**. They are commonly referred to as "pro-social" as they promote social development, tranquility and connection. These traits are also frequently described as "beta" traits, with individuals who primarily express these traits are described as "beta" as opposed to "alpha". They are also all synonymous with virtuous behaviors and if you want to be a virtuous person, you need to live, exhibit and manifest these traits and attributes.

> **Team Building**- Those skills that reduce tension, violence and anxiety. Also referred to as Relationship Skills.
> **Relationship Stability**- Those skills that serve to preserve a qualitative state. Also known as management skills.
> **Intimacy**- Those skills associated with affinity, rapport and attachment. Also identified as social maintenance and repair skills.

Skill Complexity

To help us describe in a way that is meaningful and for us to help identify specific locations on our map, we've already divided our space into a 10X10 grid, and noted that each major axis represents the major drivers of the sexual marketplace with X representing Natural Selection and Y representing Social Selection. To give us a sense of scale of what we will be talking about I think it is important that we further divided the major axes into additional grid values that we can immediately relate to regarding the level of complexity of skill sets we will be talking about in the future;

- Fundamental
- Basic
- Intermediate
- Advanced
- Refined

For the most part, this book we will not belabor the specific skill sets in any given category, other than general descriptions, as they truly become separate subjects best covered independently for detailed study, but their relationship to each other will be highly relevant.

Let's look first at the individual axes in isolation.

FUNDAMENTAL	BASIC	INTERMEDIATE	ADVANCED	REFINED

```
10 |    |    |    |    |
 9 |    |    |    |    |
 8 |    |    |    |    |
 7 |    |    |    |    |
 6 |    |    |    |    |
 5 |    |    |    |    |
 4 |    |    |    |    |
 3 |    |    |    |    |
 2 |   ===========>   |
 1 | 2 | 3 | 4 | 5 | 6 | 7 | 8 | 9 | 10
```

NATURAL SELECTION (Survival, Seduction & Provision)
PHYSICAL, SEXUAL & SOCIAL DISPLAY DIMORPHISMS

Note as we move from left to right, we are adding in level of complexity and mastery of the individual skill from simple to very complex. Also note that in the horizontal axis we are talking about Natural Selection; those traits associated with survival (physical display), provision (social display) and seduction (sexual display). At any time in which we move laterally, we are utilizing or are under the influence of Natural Selection forces. For men it's called Hypogamy. For women it's referred to as Hypergamy.

The MAP- A Personal Guide to the Sexual Marketplace

Natural Selection:

	SURVIVAL	SEDUCTION	PROVISION
HYPERGAMY	*Physical Stature*	Sexual Enticement	*Social Rank*
	Health	Sexual Provocation	*Wealth*
	Fitness	*Sexual Execution*	*Power*
			Fame
HYPOGAMY	Physical Stature	Sexual Enticement	*Youth*
	Health	Sexual Provocation	*Fertility*
	Vigor	*Sexual Accessibility*	*Variety*

Hypergamy: a natural sexual attraction predilection of females for traits and behaviors associated in males with physical stature, health, fitness (**survival dimorphisms**), social standing, rank, displays of wealth, and resources (**provisional dimorphisms**) and displays of deliberate sexual enticement, provocation and execution (**seduction dimorphisms**).

Hypogamy: a natural sexual attraction predilection of males for traits and behaviors associated in females with health, fitness and vigor (**survival dimorphisms**), youth, fertility and variety (**provisional dimorphisms**) and displays of deliberate sexual enticement, provocation and accessibility (**seduction dimorphisms**).

Likewise when we view the Social Selection axis we have an increasing value in the vertical plane, or 'Y' axis, and any time we move in the vertical plane we are utilizing or are under the influence of Social Selection forces.

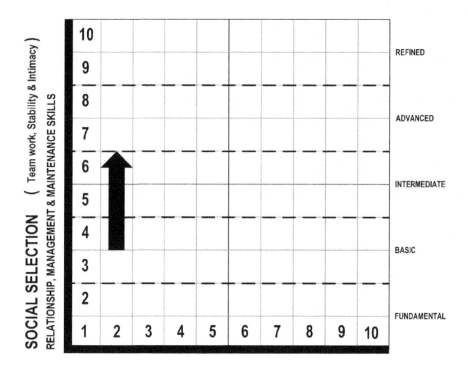

Social Selections are those behavioral dynamics that foster and develop **Team Building**, models of behavior that promote **Relationship Stability** and interactions between individuals that promote **Intimacy**.

> **Team Building-** Those skills that reduce tension, violence and anxiety; also referred to as Relationship Skills.
> **Relationship Stability-** Those skills that serve to preserve a qualitative state and assure performace; also known as management skills.
> **Intimacy-** Those skills associated with affinity, rapport and attachment; also identified as social maintenance and repair skills.

The MAP- A Personal Guide to the Sexual Marketplace

Quick Assessment

Without going into too much detail or fuss, do a quick calculation; where do you stand as far as your Natural Selection values: how well do you physically represent yourself, how well do you socially represent yourself and how well do you sexually represent yourself? Of the five categories; fundamental, basic, intermediate, advanced and refined, just pick one that is generally appropriate.

Then do the same for Social Selection; how are your relationship skills, management skills, maintenance and repair skills? Again, just select one that is generally true for you.

Based upon those two selections you should be able to find your general location somewhere on our map.

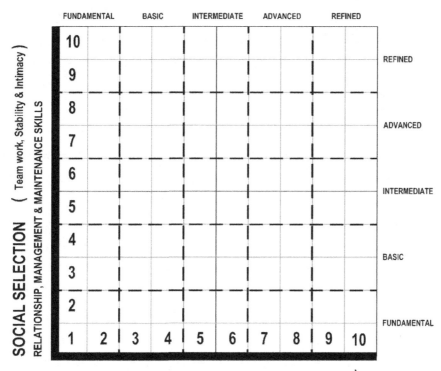

FUNDAMENTAL   BASIC   INTERMEDIATE   ADVANCED   REFINED

SOCIAL SELECTION (Team work, Stability & Intimacy)

RELATIONSHIP, MANAGEMENT & MAINTENANCE SKILLS

REFINED
ADVANCED
INTERMEDIATE
BASIC
FUNDAMENTAL

NATURAL SELECTION Survival, Seduction & Provision)
PHYSICAL, SEXUAL & SOCIAL DISPLAY DIMORPHISMS

For initial purposes we're going to assume that you occupy the whole grid that you've selected. Based on what you've selected take a look and get a feel for where you've placed yourself and why. Feel free to adjust it where you feel you might be better situated to represent where you truly are (where you are, not where you'd like to be). This is probably the first time you've seen yourself placed in the sexual marketplace. It can be an eye opener. Especially if it is terribly shifted one way or the other, but it shouldn't really come as a shock. You've already known about your general situation, as most people are relatively self-aware, and I suspect you will be too. The difference though is we are defining it and you're actually seeing it in context and to scale in relation to other factors that make up the sexual marketplace.

Based on this information, if you were to shift a grid square, what skills, attributes or behaviors should you be focusing on?

Here's a clue;

Horizontal shifts: Natural Selection; physical, social and sexual displays.

Vertical shifts: Social Selection; relationship, management, maintenance and repair skills.

Diagonal: equal proportion of Natural and Social Selection traits and attributes.

CHAPTER 2
The MAP Zones

Outliers

To help us get an intuitive feel and better understanding for our map and the drivers of the sexual marketplace let's look at the extreme borders of it, analyze a bit about the types of people that manifest these traits, attributes and their abilities, to help us understand not only their position, but how that relates to the greater environment, as well and how we fare in comparison. In doing so, we will be looking directly at the two primary drivers of the sexual marketplace; Natural selection and Social selection and how these individuals fare in both categories to place them in the sexual marketplace outlying zones (extreme positions).

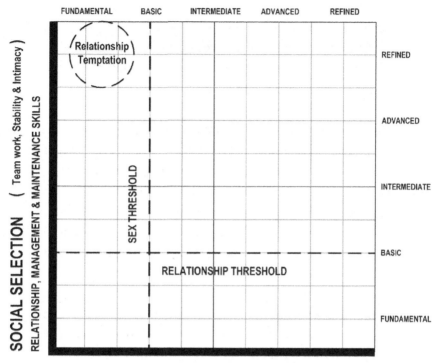

NATURAL SELECTION (Survival, Seduction & Provision)
PHYSICAL, SEXUAL & SOCIAL DISPLAY DIMORPHISMS

Outlier Group 1- Low Natural, High Social Selection

Our first group will have a tremendous asymmetrical emphasis of social selection traits, attributes and abilities within the sexual marketplace in comparison to the Natural selection.

Individuals inhabiting this area of our map exhibit the low end of the biological spectrum of natural selection (fundamental Natural Selection category). They are unfit and manifest this physically. Their posture and body language further communicate this. They may also be born with disadvantaged physical appearance of which they do little to remedy or have gained one through the course of their life, but ultimately both give all

The MAP- A Personal Guide to the Sexual Marketplace

the indications of having succumbed to it. They may present themselves in dress in similar fashion; appearances and presentation may not matter to them; they may be unkempt, ill-groomed or poorly fashioned. They are likely uninterested in social status, standing or rank and typically make up the lower rung of the social order. We also know they will be horrible at presenting themselves in a sexual manner, creating a sexual context or executing upon their sexual desires if they have any.

On the opposite end of the spectrum they rank incredibly high in pro-social, pro-relationship and virtuous behaviors (Refined Social Selection Category). They have a tremendous ability to develop and foster relationships, to collaborate and to lead teams through motivation, inspiration and mentorship; to effectively listen, understand those around them, to relate to their context and to give voice to it. They have the ability to manage individuals and these relationships through developing trust, respect and ensuring that they remain productive, viable and beneficial to the social construct involved. They also have an ability to deeply connect, resonant, and share a profound attachment of emotional sentiment, points of mutual interest and shared fascination. Because of these extreme attributes and abilities, they trigger a natural genetic pathway response of attraction and a relationship temptation response based on exhibiting three fundamental attachment developments:

- Emotional Attachment- In responding to our emotional needs, we can develop a sense of attraction based upon our having our emotional needs met. Do we feel accepted, appreciated, loved and validated for who we are and what we have to offer?
- Psychological Attachment – in serving our psychological needs, we can develop a sense of attraction based upon having our psychological needs met. Do we feel safe, secured and empowered within our circumstances? Are the voids of our psychological development (life developmental stages) being addressed, resolved or repeated?

- Intellectual Triggers Attachment- in providing to our intellectual needs, we can develop a sense of attraction based upon having our intellectual needs met. Is this individual stimulating our need or responding to a framework of thought stimulation and providing a shared sense of value?

Based on having all or any combination of our emotional, psychological and intellectual needs met, we possess a natural and biological sexual response pathway to form attachment and potentially attraction in response to the individual meeting these needs. It is one of the truly remarkable things that make us human; the multitude of pathways in which as a species can find a way to mate and propagate our kind. There is no single formula. It isn't just a case of lust, followed by attraction, then by attachment. It can be worked in reverse order, as indicated here.

The big problem though is that they absolutely reside below the sexual threshold. That is to say, on a sexual level they do not evoke any sense of lust within us, they may even repulse us sexually, regardless of how we may feel emotionally, psychologically or intellectually about them. This too, is biologically and genetically hardwired into our neurological system. We are selective breeders. We're mammals, not fish. We don't spawn. We couple and mate selectively and a fundamental process of that is the evocation of lust and desire. People who reside here manifest and exhibit neither.

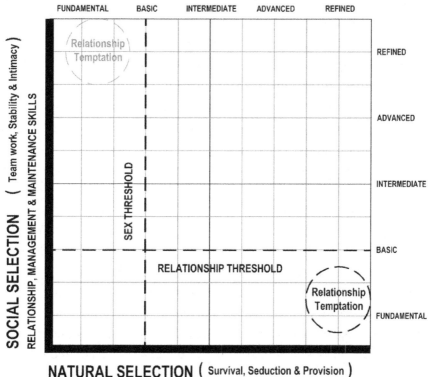

SOCIAL SELECTION (Team work, Stability & Intimacy)
RELATIONSHIP, MANAGEMENT & MAINTENANCE SKILLS

FUNDAMENTAL BASIC INTERMEDIATE ADVANCED REFINED

REFINED

ADVANCED

INTERMEDIATE

BASIC

FUNDAMENTAL

Relationship Temptation

SEX THRESHOLD

RELATIONSHIP THRESHOLD

Relationship Temptation

NATURAL SELECTION (Survival, Seduction & Provision)
PHYSICAL, SEXUAL & SOCIAL DISPLAY DIMORPHISMS

Outlier Group 2- High Natural, Low Social Selection

Our next group will again exhibit immensely asymmetrical traits, attributes and abilities within the sexual marketplace, this time with tremendous emphasis upon natural selection.

Individuals here will manifest and be exemplars of physical fitness, prowess and aesthetic visual health. It will be of almost comic book proportions in which they physically exhibit the dimorphisms of the sexes in masculine and feminine physical features. They will go to extreme lengths to not only be incredibly attractive, fit and physically powerful, their lives will center around it and be expressions of it. Likewise, they will be incredibly tied to their standing and ranking socially. Their sense of purpose, value and contribution will be directly tied to their wealth, power and attractiveness. Their sense of dress, material possessions, mannerisms and behavioral motivations will be derived in establishing, maintaining and sustaining their social rank and position. Sexually they will exude overt sexuality: lust, desire and direct, aggressive sexual enticement.

From a social selection perspective these individuals are terribly disadvantaged; they lack the empathic ability to relate or to connect to others beyond superficiality. Consequently, they have terribly poor relationship skills and abilities to defuse social tensions or anxieties. In fact, it is in their nature to provoke those, to leverage them and to exploit them. They have very limited relationship management abilities outside manipulation and exploitation; exemplified by dominance, aggression and sexual competition, provocations and ultimatums. Due to their tremendous physical attractiveness, wealth, power & influence and overt sexual command they have little to no use for maintaining or repairing existing relationships that are strained or damaged in their due course. It is far easier to dismiss, replace and recycle individuals, relationships and social environments that no longer serve their purposes. The speed and to the degree in which this takes place is stunning to behold.

Based upon the natural and biological triggers of attraction of Hypogamy and Hypergamy and how these individuals truly exhibit, express and manifest these traits, attributes and abilities, we will naturally be drawn toward the predominant sexual pathway of lust, attraction and then attachment, and as a consequence be tempted to believe they are relationship potential. This is what Natural Selection is all about, raw sexual appeal, enticement and copulation; irrespective of relationship potential. Not only that, but our biological and neurological structures are actually designed to reward us when we act on these impulses, regardless of the emotional, physical and psychological toll that may be in store for us. Sex is incredibly rewarding. Great sex is incredibly addictive. Great sex with highly attractive and sexualized people is overwhelmingly personally validating. It is at the center of our biological imperative to do so. When we do so, we are acquiescing to our nature, which makes it so terribly powerful, commanding and stubborn.

The problem occurs when on a social and personal level we face the reality that this biological system is geared toward a single mating cycle, if that (especially for people here). For humans, this mating cycle is approximately four years; the time it takes to find, acquire, copulate, birth and rear an infant to toddler development, prior to repeating this cycle with a new mating partner. This is true for both men and women, as current anthropological, psychological and sociological research collaborates and confirms. Individuals that only have a fundamental ability to establish, manage, maintain and sustain relationships show themselves immediately or in short enough order that they remain below the relationship threshold and do not rise above.

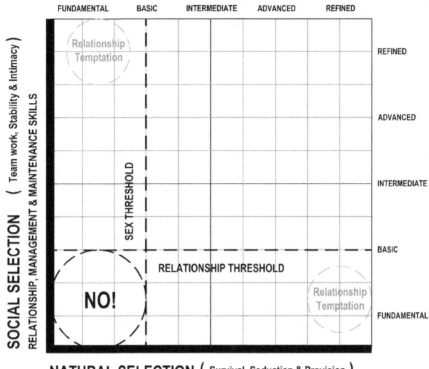

FUNDAMENTAL   BASIC   INTERMEDIATE   ADVANCED   REFINED

Relationship Temptation

REFINED

ADVANCED

INTERMEDIATE

SEX THRESHOLD

BASIC

RELATIONSHIP THRESHOLD

NO!

Relationship Temptation

FUNDAMENTAL

SOCIAL SELECTION (Team work, Stability & Intimacy)
RELATIONSHIP, MANAGEMENT & MAINTENANCE SKILLS

NATURAL SELECTION (Survival, Seduction & Provision)
PHYSICAL, SEXUAL & SOCIAL DISPLAY DIMORPHISMS

Outlier Group 3- Low Natural, Low Social Selection

Our third group is a special one in many ways. These individuals score incredibly low in both the natural and social selection traits, attributes and abilities and not by choice, but by circumstances beyond their control. In all likelihood, they are developmentally disabled or have suffered physical trauma resulting in a devastating alteration of their lives. Because these individuals suffer significantly from impaired intellectual and adaptive functionality, they are a protected class of people; morally, ethically and legally and we will treat and consider them as such. These truly are God's children. They deserve our compassion, consideration and respect. As such, this is truly an out of bounds area of the sexual marketplace. We will

The MAP- A Personal Guide to the Sexual Marketplace

not go here. We will not engage people in this realm in any sexual manner, under any circumstances. When we do, we are acting criminally, immorally and unethically and deserve to be appropriately identified as sexual predators subject to social ostracization and punishment to the full extent of the law.

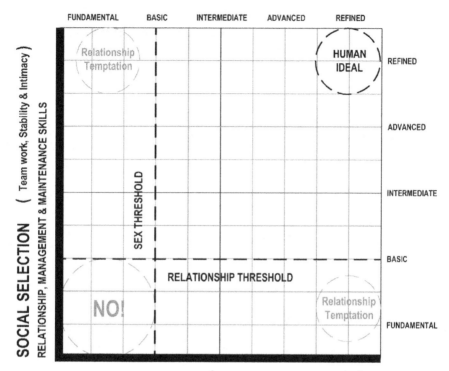

NATURAL SELECTION (Survival, Seduction & Provision)
PHYSICAL, SEXUAL & SOCIAL DISPLAY DIMORPHISMS

Outlier Group 4- High Natural, High Social Selection

Our last group represents not the human potential, but the human ideal actualized in equally maximizing both the natural and social selection drivers of the sexual marketplace; they are fit, healthy and attractive individuals, who effortlessly are able to make deep connections with people, reduce their social anxieties and have meaningful rapport with those around them. Their social standing and rank is attributed to the value and significance of which they bring to people's lives, as they are able to effectively manage a network of relationships effectively, in a mutually supportive, healthy and beneficial manner. Where there is strain and conflict, they are able to resolve it by finding the underpinning failed

The MAP- A Personal Guide to the Sexual Marketplace

expectations, with an approach that develops greater awareness, understanding and connection between the parties. Lastly, they are in full command of their sexuality and sexualized selves: in interest, expression and in response. These are people we should aspire to be. These are the people who we have the potential of becoming.

The Map Zones

Now that we have an idea and understanding of the extreme ranges of our map and the sexual marketplace, let's begin to start to identify the spaces and associated zones in-between and adjacent to these outlier poles, and what they can start to really tell us about the sexual marketplace and your position within it. Note that we have also identified two critical thresholds within the sexual market: the sex threshold and the relationship threshold. If you are below these no one is likely to engage you for these activities. Think of these as minimum standards for our species. I personally think they're rather generous and set a rather low bar for humanity, but then again, our species has thrived because of it. With that being said, we're going to try to raise the bar and look out for your best interests and we're going to avoid shopping for a partner and mate at the dollar store of human existence. Also, please note that individual standards, bars, values et., vary. Our graph and map is a general representation. Your personal map may very well have differing values and thresholds. That's OK. Just realize that and understand the implications of such as you reflect upon your map as we move forward.

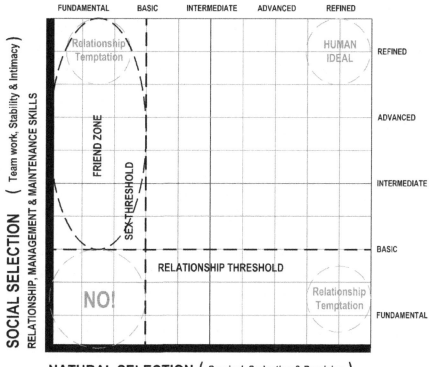

FUNDAMENTAL   BASIC   INTERMEDIATE   ADVANCED   REFINED

SOCIAL SELECTION (Team work, Stability & Intimacy)

RELATIONSHIP, MANAGEMENT & MAINTENANCE SKILLS

Relationship Temptation

HUMAN IDEAL — REFINED

— ADVANCED

FRIEND ZONE

SEX-THRESHOLD

— INTERMEDIATE

— BASIC

RELATIONSHIP THRESHOLD

NO!

Relationship Temptation

— FUNDAMENTAL

NATURAL SELECTION (Survival, Seduction & Provision)

PHYSICAL, SEXUAL & SOCIAL DISPLAY DIMORPHISMS

Friend Zone

The Friend Zone is probably without doubt the most famous and talked about of the zones. It is also the only zone in which we've all faced, each and every one of us during our adolescence and beyond. People who are here are below the sex threshold. For teenagers, that's an appropriate place to be, as being highly sexualized at a young age is neither beneficial for them (wrecks their lives) or society on a whole. Cultures that promote or foster sexualized children are in rapidly advancing in decay. For active, healthy adults, the friend zone is a painful, soul-crushing and doubt-casting region in which to exist. For both groups they are here for the same reasons:

The MAP- A Personal Guide to the Sexual Marketplace

- Physical status- you don't look or sub-communicate the part of a sexually confident grown individual. For children and teenagers this is just straight up biology and should not be rushed (be patient). For adults it is a series of health, lifestyle and developmental issues that are at play.
- Social status- you lack standing and value to the social group in which you're involved. For teenagers this is most likely due to under-developed social and relationship skills. For adults it is those, plus a failure to meet or exceed additional societal expectations of a viable adult or mate.
- Sexual status- you're weak in identifying and presenting Indicators of Interest or IOIs (those behavior traits of flirtation, teasing and banter that signal sexual interest). You're likely ignorant or unskilled in the principals of sexual escalation and you definitely have difficulty in actually closing the sexual deal. You just can't manage to pull the trigger or you bungle it.

For teenagers this whole story here is about adolescence and is a naturally terrifying and uncomfortable place to be and to transfer through. For adults it's debilitating. It is also signaling that you haven't either picked up on these life lessons and skills or that you haven't mastered them to the degree you need to in order to prevent being friend zoned. The point of all this is to recognize that if you're here, you're here for a reason and that you play a very strong hand in that reasoning. Even among dating professionals (professional pickup-artists) I don't know a single one who wasn't adversely affected by their experiences transitioning through this phase, but each of them turned to face their weakness, emotional trauma and psychological underpinnings and decided to take significant and massive action to rectify it. The best of them utilize those experiences in empathic and sympathetic ways to teach others how to avoid those experiences and transition into being vibrant sexual adults. If others have done it before you, you can too.

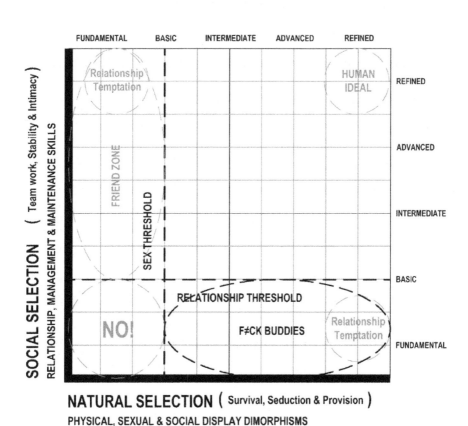

FUNDAMENTAL   BASIC   INTERMEDIATE   ADVANCED   REFINED

SOCIAL SELECTION (Team work, Stability & Intimacy)
RELATIONSHIP, MANAGEMENT & MAINTENANCE SKILLS

Relationship Temptation

HUMAN IDEAL — REFINED

— ADVANCED

FRIEND ZONE

SEX THRESHOLD

— INTERMEDIATE

— BASIC

RELATIONSHIP THRESHOLD

NO!

F#CK BUDDIES

Relationship Temptation

— FUNDAMENTAL

NATURAL SELECTION (Survival, Seduction & Provision)
PHYSICAL, SEXUAL & SOCIAL DISPLAY DIMORPHISMS

Fuck Buddies

If the Friend Zone was the most famous, the Fuck Buddy Zone is without question the most infamous. This is the opposite end of the Friend Zone, people here are having sex and in a significant way. In scandalous ways.

The MAP- A Personal Guide to the Sexual Marketplace

Just like the people in the Friend Zone are not getting laid for a reason, the people here are getting laid for the opposite reason; they look the part, they act the part and they have little to no problem with sexual display, enticement, escalation, closing and executing sexually.

This is the realm typified by douchebags and party- girls. Because there is so much to be gained in regard to self-worth, self-respect and social and cultural validation with being fit, attractive, and highly sexual, there's little motivation to be virtuous; that is, to develop pro-social, pro-relationship skills, pro-relationship management abilities, pro-relationship maintenance aptitudes or pro-relationship repair proficiencies. It is far easier, more economical and a far more efficient utilization of your time, energy and resources to recycle and replace faulty relationships and personal involvements. For some, and it is a major tenant of the Pickup Industry, you actually want to refrain from virtuous behaviors to intentionally mitigate the hassles, nuances and complexities of having to actually engage the same individual repeatedly, even in marginal relationship structures. Their hallmark is a one-off sale; a relatively low-quality product and service being sold with no intent of repeat business aka disposable sexuality. This is true for both men and women - the primary value of the relationship being peddled is sexual.

The individuals that reside here are all below the relationship threshold because they lack the ability or desire to relate, establish, maintain or sustain relationships in any meaningful manner.

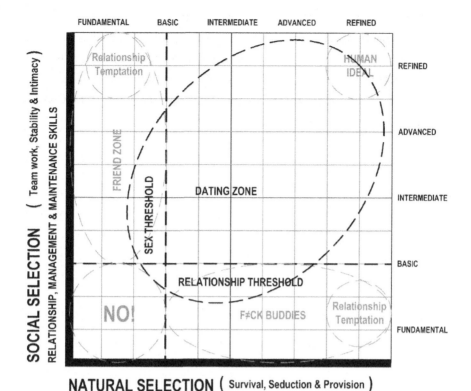

FUNDAMENTAL   **BASIC**   **INTERMEDIATE**   **ADVANCED**   **REFINED**

SOCIAL SELECTION (Team work, Stability & Intimacy)
RELATIONSHIP, MANAGEMENT & MAINTENANCE SKILLS

Relationship Temptation

HUMAN IDEAL   REFINED

FRIEND ZONE

SEX THRESHOLD

DATING ZONE

ADVANCED

INTERMEDIATE

BASIC

RELATIONSHIP THRESHOLD

NO!

F#CK BUDDIES

Relationship Temptation

FUNDAMENTAL

NATURAL SELECTION (Survival, Seduction & Provision)
PHYSICAL, SEXUAL & SOCIAL DISPLAY DIMORPHISMS

Dating Zone

This enormous zone is the Dating Zone. It's the largest and most encompassing zone within our map - and it should be. This is the zone of the pool of individuals who make up the dating environment. I happen to believe that all well-adjusted, healthy, socially responsible people should make up this segment of our society and population. These people should be datable. They may not float your particular boat, but they are datable. I believe that normal people are datable, and we can see "normal" in the center of our map: the location of value (5,5) for both natural selection and social selection. I've highlighted the cross hairs of normalcy on our map, and the two lines that bifurcate the words "Dating Zone" in the diagram above. We should be inside of this zone. This is where we want to be. This

The MAP- A Personal Guide to the Sexual Marketplace

zone should be the natural make up of mankind, and if it isn't something is wrong. Notice that generally speaking "normal" isn't dead center of our dating population pool; it can't be, as we've eliminated much of what falls below normal just to get to the caliber of people that make up the dating pool. Note there's tremendous value beyond the center, effectively skewing our zone. This will be important later on.

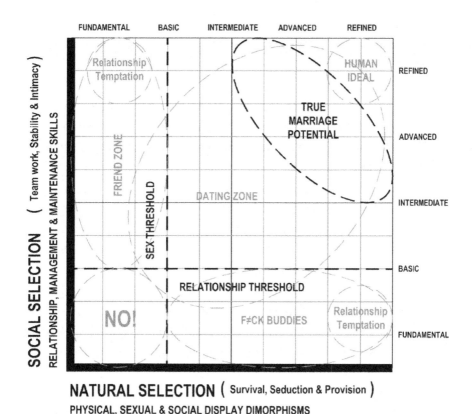

FUNDAMENTAL   BASIC   INTERMEDIATE   ADVANCED   REFINED

SOCIAL SELECTION (Team work, Stability & Intimacy)
RELATIONSHIP, MANAGEMENT & MAINTENANCE SKILLS

Relationship Temptation

HUMAN IDEAL — REFINED

FRIEND ZONE

SEX THRESHOLD

TRUE MARRIAGE POTENTIAL — ADVANCED

DATING ZONE — INTERMEDIATE

BASIC

RELATIONSHIP THRESHOLD

NO!

F#CK BUDDIES

Relationship Temptation — FUNDAMENTAL

NATURAL SELECTION (Survival, Seduction & Provision)
PHYSICAL, SEXUAL & SOCIAL DISPLAY DIMORPHISMS

Marriage Potential

Of all the zones this is my favorite; this is the Marriage Potential Zone. This is the zone of people who give a shit about themselves, others, the relationships they have and the social networks they help foster and create. These individuals are above average in both of our sexual marketplace categories of natural selection and social selection; they look, act, dress and behave the part of a viable and responsible sexual partner. They also can establish, maintain, sustain and repair the relationships they are in. It isn't that they are perfect or ideal. Rather, it's that they are without major flaw and they've worked hard to get that way. This level and caliber of person doesn't just occur, they're created. They are people who've made

The MAP- A Personal Guide to the Sexual Marketplace

something of themselves. Some will have had the immense benefits of having parents and a social and cultural make up that promote these behaviors. Others face far more difficult realities in achieving this standing and should be celebrated for having done so. It's a significant achievement, and it is a reality that is available to each of us.

Now you can choose to commit to anyone anywhere on this map. That is your choice, but I don't think it is wise. I believe you should be aiming to become the type of person who resides in the Marriage Potential Zone and only allocate your time, energy, focus, desire and resources to people in this realm. These are virtuous people, exhibiting virtuous traits, attributes and abilities. They live virtuous lives. I believe if we want to live in a virtuous world we have the responsibility to reward and promote virtue. Committing our energy, time, focus and value outside of this isn't rewarding virtue. We cannot claim to be virtuous when we disengage from virtuous behavior. And when we do we're betraying virtue. We're traitors to virtue and we know it. We don't like it said. We don't like it brought up and we don't want to be reminded of it, but it's there. We can't hide from ourselves. We know we could have done differently, we could have chose differently and we could have been rewarded differently because of it.

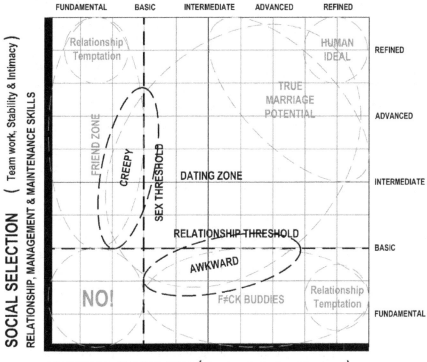

NATURAL SELECTION (Survival, Seduction & Provision)
PHYSICAL, SEXUAL & SOCIAL DISPLAY DIMORPHISMS

Creepy and Awkward Zones

There two significant zones we haven't talked about yet. These are the two areas that lay between the Friend Zone, the Dating Zone and the Fuck Buddy Zone; the Creepy Zone and the Awkward Zone. These are not so much zones as truly obstacles to normalcy. They are the hurdles people face just prior to becoming normalized adults. And both are the relative equivalent of earning a 'D' in either Natural Selection (you're awkward) and/or Social Selection (you're creepy). In both conditions you haven't quite failed, which would have gotten you dismissed, but instead you haven't quite passed the test of having command over the basics of life.

It should be readily recognized that life is vastly more difficult without social skills. Likewise, romantic and sexual relationships are next to impossible

The MAP- A Personal Guide to the Sexual Marketplace

without the ability to appropriately express yourself in a sensual, sexual and receptive manner. The incongruence of behaviors, actions, beliefs, abilities and attributes all create tension where there is an expectation of competency but there is none to be found. This is what is meant when we are "creepy" or "awkward". We are manifesting incongruent behaviors. An inappropriate handling of a specific social situation, being socially or sexually inexperienced, failing to recognize appropriate context for given behaviors or actions, being immature in our relationship management and sustainment abilities, "trying too hard" and "being fake" to the point that our insecurities peek out through our false façade of confidence and competency are all examples of being creepy or awkward.

As I've brought up previously, if you're a teenager, this is a normal rite of passage to adulthood. It can expected and should be expected and can be worked out as part and parcel of growing up into a functional adult over the course of your high school years and a couple beyond that.

For the rest of us, it signals that there is a significant deficiency in our development regarding either of these selection processes and should be a wakeup call to do something about it or willfully acknowledge our failure, embrace it and succumb to it without further complaint. I think that would be a terrible life choice and as such I'm here to help.

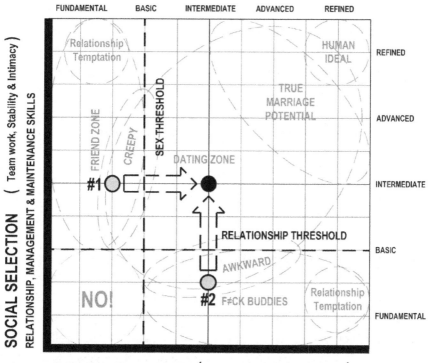

Map Utilization

This is the fun part. We can start to make use of our map and how that will specifically start to pertain to you. Now that we have a good understanding of not only the primary drivers of the sexual marketplace, we understand also the context in which we start to segment this context into major value zones and recognize that the transitions between zones creates tensions associated with incongruency of association between the two. Previously

The MAP- A Personal Guide to the Sexual Marketplace

we were able to identify our location within the sexual marketplace by cross coordinating between the average of our Natural Selection values: physical, social and sexual display dimorphisms and our Social Selection values: relationship, management and maintenance skills.

Unlike previously where we didn't have the value overlays associated with the various zones (because those zones contain inherent value and we have a natural tendency to resist reality when it is something we'd rather not face or admit to), now we do. We can see ourselves squarely within any given zone. If we are uncomfortable with our positioning, we need to first stop resisting this reality. Resisting reality only brings on misery. Misery which we can control. Furthermore, if we can't be honest with ourselves, we cannot be honest with others, our dealings with them and understanding their responses to us. Acceptance of a reality is our first objective in overcoming it.

Likewise, in our previous exercise we didn't identify where were really heading. We were only looking at shifting grids in general and what attributes would lead to that. While still true, now our shifts are based on concrete value objectives: reaching the dating zone, marriage potential or even the human ideal. Often, we try to fool ourselves by saying one thing but meaning another. We say we want to date a nice guy/gal, but really, emotionally, mean we want someone of marriage potential and we're looking specifically for the human ideal. There's nothing inherently wrong with that, other than not recognizing the significance and implications of desiring these outcomes. Are we prepared or preparing ourselves to meet them considering the magnitude of our objectives? Typically, we know we are not and the difference between our expectations and reality is the measurement of our dissatisfaction. This dissatisfaction plays out, most critically non-verbally. Unhappy, bitter and resentful people sub-communicate this inner world via their behaviors and actions, as do happy, genial and kind individuals, but with vastly differing outcomes. By being honest with ourselves about the true nature of our objectives we can acknowledge the magnitude of our objectives in the light of reality in which they exist. We will no longer be deluding ourselves into thinking they are any less than what they really are, and we need to accept that we will have to rise up to meet them.

The vector between where we are and where we want to go is important to understanding the nature of the skill sets, attributes and traits we are lacking or failing to display. We must identify, know and understand what those are if we are to correct or overcome them. Focusing on skill sets, attributes and traits that are not in alignment with our objective will not get us to where we want to go. You simply can't get there by going somewhere else.

I believe people understand this on an intuitive level but become incredibly entrenched when viewing the direction they must go under the auspices of the sexual marketplace and its primary drivers of Natural Selection and Social Selection. I can sympathize with this, part of it is simply human behavior. We want to focus on our strengths while avoiding our weaknesses, but doing so doesn't help us in the long run. We remain weak where we are weakest. It's one thing to be talking about getting into physical shape and exercising to respond to the Natural Selection driver of physical dimorphisms, but where do you go to work out, social and sexual dimorphisms? This takes people not only out of their comfort zone. Compounding this there are often aware of only a few outlets to get information on coaching, support or mentorship for improving socially and, unfortunately, much of it they will consider out of the mainstream of cultural acceptance. For the most part, they probably just haven't thought about it much either, which doesn't help. The most resistant people to accepting the sexual marketplace for what it is, the drivers that make it up and consequently those that can have the greatest impact on their lives have deep seated beliefs to the contrary and cling to these beliefs despite all evidence to the contrary. I'm not here to argue with those people. In many ways they are right. They should be good enough the way they are, but then again, they should be equally accepting of their results. Wishing things were different from what they are doesn't change the way things are.

The MAP- A Personal Guide to the Sexual Marketplace

We have to work in concert with reality if we are to achieve our aims and avoid considerable misery in the process.

Another part of avoiding misery is to recognize the actual context of that reality. Most people don't take the time to evaluate the context of what they are trying to achieve. In our examples of both the Friend Zone and the Fuck Buddy Zone, they both have between fundamental and basic skill sets, attributes or abilities that they wish to improve upon to the level of intermediate or average. This is terribly important; they are not looking to have advanced or refined skill levels. On the contrary they're both looking to be "normal" or average. On the whole, this shouldn't be much of a challenge. Sure there's work involved, but it's not monumental and the skill levels involved all reside along the basic to early intermediate range. Focusing on advanced or refined skills is not really going to help them out. It isn't what they really need.

The second part of this is to identify and recognize what obstacles they will be facing, when they will face them and when they can be expected to be beyond them. In each of their cases they are already on the near side of either the Creepy Zone or the Awkward Zone and will require a degree of work to get past this area. As such, they can expect that one, they are already facing direct adversity and challenges and two, that they will face additional challenges moving forward and three, that after a short work effort they will be on the far side of this zone facing little resistance moving forward into the dating zone. If we know that we are going to have the most difficulties and challenges early into our journey, we can and should prepare ourselves for this. Part of this will simply be acknowledging the challenges to reduce the pressure, another is the need to have greater motivation to instigate change and lastly to recognize the importance of real change, when it occurs, to continue to fuel this progress and continued work ahead.

Work efficiency management studies have routinely showcased the importance between the value differentiation of the impact a "negative" has over a "positive". While the studies vary in intensity of the resultants, they generally conform to a rule that a negative is four times as value laden as a similar positive. That's huge! A 400% increase in value based on a negative occurrence. How is this fact relevant? Well if we are looking to be more work efficient we should probably start with implementing policies and procedures that will garner the most effective benefits for the least cost. That means focusing squarely on the "negative" and specifically on their removal. Removing a single negative will have four times the impact of improving an existing factor or adding a new one into the equation. How does this help you? Well, when was the last time someone was willing to say openly that you could achieve 400% better results (four times) if you just got out of your own god damn way!? Really! If we just stopped getting in our own way we'd have vastly better results.

Now, let's talk specifics. It's not just any thing you're doing that gets in your way, but the specific elements that reside along the line between you and your objective. What are they? Take time to think specifically about what axis of development (Natural Selection or Social Selection) that you need to work on and first examine how you are an active agent in limiting that development. How would things change if you limited, reduced or stopped those elements? Do you know what it is or how many there are? The more you identify here and are able to augment and limit the better. For the individuals in our two examples, I would say that if they did just this step alone that they would likely clear the Creep and Awkward Zones outright! How's that for effectiveness and immediate improvement? This is to say that people in both these zones are actively doing things that are placing themselves there and preventing them from being in the zone of normalcy.

> One of the most fundamental failures that individuals in either the Friend Zone or Fuck Buddy Zone is that hold two complimentary self-concepts; they believe that they belong in that zone i.e. that they do not hold self-merit beyond either limiting zone and the second is that others will always feel the same way regarding them. A third concept is that the past will forever define who and what

they are. Seneca stated something to the effect that we suffer more in imagination than in reality. Sometimes we need to just get over ourselves and our past to create the future we would like to assume. A serious re-orientation and perspective regarding yourself is a foundational step.

Once we've identified our self-limiting factors, what are the under-pinning skill sets, attributes or traits that support these?

People in the Friend Zone tend to significantly lack social skills associated with engaging those of the opposite sex. Learning to open a conversation (initiate it), hold eye contact when talking, having a simple conversation and expressing self-confidence when doing so is crucial to understand and develop. And much like working out, it is a process over an extended period of time that develops the result, not a given workout. If you want to be fit, muscular and a social Adonis you are going to have to work those social muscles out. You're going to have to lift hard, lift often to failure, sweat and leave your self-pity on the floor.

For those in the Fuck Buddy Zone you command a disproportionate level of biological and socially innate Natural Selection traits and attributes associated with physical beauty, social charm and influence while exhibiting a strong command of sexual enticement, arousal and sexual talent. Unfortunately, emphasis of Natural Selection traits is not a relationship strategy, they are a mating and sexual strategy. These strengths do not promote, sustain and maintain relationships. They are geared toward creating and stimulating sexual arousal and attention, which may lead to the desire for a relationship, but these are not the traits involved in fostering and supporting relationships successfully long term. One of the fastest ways a woman can signal to men that she belongs in the Fuck Buddy Zone, is to actively promote it; clearly identify and place yourself as not being relationship material from the get go.

The MAP- A Personal Guide to the Sexual Marketplace

Say things like "you're crazy", or qualify it that you're "a nice girl, but, don't piss me off because you have pocket full of crazy". My two favorites are that you identify as being a feminist ('strong independent woman') or that "your children mean everything to you", but you divorced their father because you "weren't happy".

Without a doubt those are the areas that need to see additional shoring up of support, because we know them to be weak. Putting forth a conscious effort to re-familiarize ourselves with and improve these skills is our second step to self-improvement. These will not be new skills or abilities, but already established ones that we are looking to cement a solid foundation on, prior to making additional advancements or improvements. Doing so is effective and efficient because they are already known, you have familiarity with them and they will help build an honest motivational momentum of success.

What are they? Develop a personal list and start to break those categories down into small actionable steps. What research can you do to read up on them, to improve and trigger conscious action for utilization? Then, are you actively acting on this awareness and knowledge? Specifically target a given element and go out and exercise it based upon your research. If you need to learn to be social, going out and just passing people and saying "Hi" is a great first step. If you're in the Fuck Buddy Zone and you desire a relationship, how about communicating that above the unflattering chip on your shoulder you call 'Independence'. Nothing solidifies comprehension as actually doing the task rather than just reading or watching a video. We have to actually train for the results we want or expect. Professionals call this re-current training and it's every bit as essential to them, as it will be to us.

Once we've gotten out of our own way by eliminating detrimental behavior and improving existing skills do we look to then identify new skills or advance our skill sets beyond the level basic level. This may be a bit challenging, as we'll need to identify them and we may not know what they are. This means we may have to go looking for them. We may have to ask others to see things in an objective light that we may not see for ourselves and nowhere is this more challenging than when we are looking to see ourselves. In these cases, we can look to see things in either their absence or wake. In what either occurred or didn't occur. We may have to experiment, to test things out and learn from our experiences. This is where having trusted friends, advisors and mentors pay huge dividends. Again, all this plays to the question of where you are in the spectrum of things. Basic and fundamental skills are going to be well known, documented and readily identified. Refined and advanced skills are going to be more difficult to ascertain. Make sure to link your improvement and advancements to the experience stage appropriate to your objective. Focusing on refined skill sets isn't going to help you much, if you don't have basic and intermediate skill level abilities to support them.

To summarize and to assist those that don't want to be burdened by the lengthy explanation of the above text:

- Identify honestly where you are on The Map.
- Determine truly where you want to go.
- Recognize the realm and scale of your undertaking and prepare yourself (what classification of skills are we talking about, and how big and complex of an undertaking).
- Connect the two points- the vector tells you what skills you need to be developing on what axis.
- Identify what obstacles are present and when we should first expect them and secondly when we will be past them.
- Remove the negatives first- what are you doing to hold yourself back?
- Recurrent fundamental training -work the basics first; they are the easiest and early success will help develop motivational momentum based on real success.
- Increase your skills (along the developmental stages) - advanced skills won't help you if you possess hollowed abilities or harbor weak supporting structures.

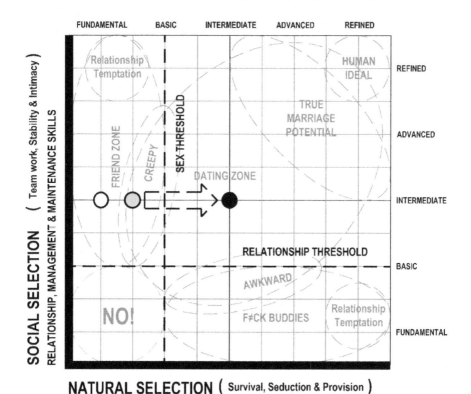

FUNDAMENTAL   BASIC   INTERMEDIATE   ADVANCED   REFINED

SOCIAL SELECTION (Team work, Stability & Intimacy)
RELATIONSHIP, MANAGEMENT & MAINTENANCE SKILLS

NATURAL SELECTION (Survival, Seduction & Provision)
PHYSICAL, SEXUAL & SOCIAL DISPLAY DIMORPHISMS

Friend Zone

If you're here, you know it. We all know it. This is one of those areas where you can't hide from others, let alone yourself. People sub-communicate the zone that they know they're in, almost blaringly. For starters, you're below the sex threshold. Others have no interest in having sex with you, you have no desire for sex where you're actually involved (real world, not fantasy) or a good combination of both. If you are here, there is no shortage of reasons as to why. Take any of the subcategories of Natural Selection; physical display, social display or sexual display and take the first five attributes, traits or features from each of them that you can think of and I'll bet you're the antithesis of each of them. That would be 15 solid reasons why you're failing on a Natural Selection Scale. It's not just a single reason. That's a pretty shitty thing to say. It really is. But the predicament is it is also all too terribly true. The problem is, my assessment isn't the worst of it. The worst of it is at the center of each of these issues in which you're directly involved. You're here because of the things you've either done or failed to do and therefore manifest these attributes. Of course, there will be those individuals that are truly outliers, where my comments above don't pertain in any fair sense. They won't pertain because the person is an outlier and outliers by their very nature shouldn't be grouped when talking about the average. Statistically speaking, they should be tossed out and reviewed later with an emphasis toward their specific concerns, but even they could probably utilize a good dose of the following:

- Physical dimorphisms- you don't look or sub-communicate the part of a sexually confident grown individual. This is due to a series of health, lifestyle and developmental issues that are overtly visible. Physically you are a negative outlier of the general population and are not engaged in the sexual marketplace because of it.
- Sexual dimorphisms - You're not even showing up to the game. You're simply not ready, prepared or presented to play. You don't exhibit nor spark sexual attention, interest or arousal. You're weak in identifying and presenting Indicators of Interest (IOIs); those behavior traits of flirtation, teasing and banter that signal sexual interest and receptivity (as opposed to intent). You're likely ignorant or unskilled in the principals of sexual escalation and you definitely have difficulty in actually closing the sexual deal (actual intent). You just can't manage to pull the trigger, or you bungle it if you even try.
- Social dimorphisms - you lack standing and value to the social group in which you're involved. This is due to under-developed social expression of personal value and a failure to meet or exceed the societal expectations of a viable adult or mate. Even if you do possess these traits, you don't manifest them.

You are largely passive and unresponsive socially. You simply lack presence, confidence and standing as a result.

That is a brutal assessment and an unforgiving one. They're all true. We both know it. I'd be lying, via omission, if I didn't acknowledge it. That doesn't mean there isn't compassion behind my telling you. I'm telling you, so we can drag these issues from under the veil of civility, so we can then address and resolve them in a beneficial manner. Keep in mind we cannot resolve that which we do not acknowledge- avoidance isn't a solution.

Fundamental Level:
At a fundamental level (true friend zone-to the left of the creepy zone) all of these dimorphisms have a common unifying link in the form of confidence or a lack thereof. If our first order of business toward self-improvement is to remove the negatives first (because they are so value laden), then we have to recognize our greatest impairment at this level is a lack of self-confidence, self-worth and self-respect. There can be any number of reasons why this is true, but uncovering those reasons isn't the focus or purpose of this book. The purpose is to point you in the right direction to go and find out for yourself. One of the most prominent reasons for a lack of self-esteem, self-worth and self-respect, is that you missed the appropriate opportunities to develop it naturally through your childhood. No parent is perfect and therefore we all will go through life having to fill those voids in our personal development. Some of us have regrettably faced undue hardships and great trauma in the course of our upbringing or lack thereof. I'm truly sorry for those individuals where that is the case, but as adults, our lives are our responsibility. Our job is to resolve our own deficiencies. Likewise, most of us have been terribly hurt by others in the course of our lives. Tales of adolescence and high school experiences are fraught with them, as we should expect, as this is the period in which we transition from children into adults. This is the growth period in which, if we've missed, failed or inadequately advanced, we must re-address appropriately. Because of the emotional traumas we've experienced here, we carry the emotional damage with us for life unless we heal those wounds and

The MAP- A Personal Guide to the Sexual Marketplace

overcome them. Although we can respond to our own emotional wounds ourselves, seeking a professionally trained and experienced health service professional can have a profound effect on accelerating your healing and can be a resource for your continued development. Having a guide that can assist you in shifting thought and behavioral patterns that are blocking and limiting your happiness and personal enrichment, freeing yourself from the patterns of anxiety, depression and self-criticism, as well as finding ways to handle resulting suffering related to trauma to prevent anger, resentment and loathing can only lead to a better, more fulfilled, thriving you.

Basic Level:

At a basic level (primarily the creepy zone) all of these dimorphisms also have a common unifying link in the form of a lack of certainty. This lack of certainty usually stems directly from a lack of confidence and experience, either from an initial lack of experience, or as a consequence of those early experiences aided by your belief of others perceptions, that took root and grew into your conceptualized belief system of yourself. From personal experience I can tell you, I don't know of a single pickup artist (PUA) or dating coach worth their salt that didn't have one of these two experiences that was significant enough for them to take massive action to rectify, often directing the course of their lives as a consequence. In fact, the best of them leverage this personal experience to relate with their clients in their teaching, coaching and development of mentorships programs.

For women, I have no doubt similar experiences shape their lives in a similar manner. In fact, I think women are more adversely affected in comparison because women develop sexual value much earlier than males. This development, or the expectation of this development, places not only a tremendous amount of pressure on a developing girl, but the extreme tenderness of age plays a critical factor in developing a sense of self-worth and particularly body image based on these biological and then socially driven factors. When beauty and sex are the primary cultural values for which an entire gender gets validation and acceptance, and you have those resources placed in the hands of an immature novice undergoing a tremendous hormonal change toward fueling adult sexuality, these values can turn into weapons that cut and wound not just girls and women themselves but boys and men as well.

Regardless of which gender we speak of, if we are to develop certainty with regard to the Natural Selection dimorphisms we are going to have to redirect and replace those earlier missing or failed experiences with healthy and affirming experiences that confidence then naturally flows from. And you thought adolescence was hard the first time? Wait until you try revisiting those situations as an adult when you have so much more at emotional stake and even more built up past history for reference.

Developing Natural Selection Traits & Attributes
While I cannot tailor an action program specifically to each of my readers individually, we can revisit each of the Natural Selection dimorphisms with the specific intent upon providing enough content that you can choose between them where you feel you will garner the most benefits in comparison to your effort and serve as an initial spring board for further self-directed research and pursuit. The two key traits we are looking to improve upon in all of the Natural Selection subcategories (Physical, Social & Sexual display dimorphisms) are confidence and certainty. The more you are unconfident and uncertain about yourself, the more I'll be unconfident and uncertain about you. So will everyone else. The greater my lack of confidence and certainty the more I'll dismiss you and try to put as much distance as I can between us. I just won't want you around, because your lack of confidence and certainty of yourself creates social tension and nobody likes tension. So regardless of the natural selection subcategory you're working on improving, keep confidence and certainty at the core of it.

Physical Display Dimorphisms- both sexes overwhelming favor and are attracted and aroused by individuals that are physically fit, healthy and have physical stature. There's no getting over this. If you are obese, you are significantly disadvantaged in the sexual marketplace, plain and simple. I'm not going to say fitness is the sole factor, because it isn't, but on a visceral and biological level it commands and commands heavily. Moving your BMI (body mass index) toward average will do wonders. It is also one of the most time consuming, energy expending and difficult things you will do. Many of you us would have to move heaven and earth just to get to a normal BMI. In order to do so, it is likely you are going to have to reconfigure your entire life because your body is a reflection of your life. No doubt both are out of control, with your body being a reflection of your life. You may also have to challenge or change deeply held belief systems associated with nutrition, exercise, and recovery protocols and behaviors. Not only that, but the changes may take an extremely long time to show visible results, which can lead to an incredibly high recidivism rate. With all that being said, you can work around body weight issues with increased focus and emphasis on the other two Natural Selection traits (social & sexual). Men here are at a greater advantage, as women don't rate a man's fitness and physical stature nearly with the same emphasis as males do women (differences between Hypergamy and Hypogamy), which we will see more of, but suffice it to say a reduction to a normal BMI will work wonders for your sexual market value. An interesting note is that for most individuals, a 20lb weight loss was visible to others. Segmenting your weight loss goals toward milestones that reflect these observable transitions can help build critical momentum to sustain your drive.

For those at the low BMI end of the spectrum there will be challenges as well, but in this culture, it is vastly more preferable to be too thin rather than too heavy. That doesn't mean you shouldn't or wouldn't benefit from a healthy lean mass gain program associated with resistance training. This option is becoming increasingly more popular and common for both men and women. They can take advantage of the continued social and cultural shift of a sense of beauty from "skinny" toward "fit" while reaping tremendous health benefits in doing so. The drawback of course is that to gain mass you're going to have to increase your feeding in proportion to the work out demands and sustainment levels. Just as a dieter has to face going hungry, you skinny bastards and bitches are going to have to eat up. Luckily

The MAP- A Personal Guide to the Sexual Marketplace

for you, you're working in a natural direction; the more you work out, the hungrier you get. Not so in dieting (yeah, I'm personally pissed about this).

For both groups and both genders being actively engaged in a fitness protocol results in the positive Natural Selection traits of fitness, stature and vigor. While you may in fact be out of shape and unhealthy, your posture and displayed energy levels will be improved remarkably enough for others to take note and respond in a more receptive manner.

Social Display Dimorphisms- is the most complex of the three categories; as men and women evolutionarily faced differing adversities and challenges based on our differing biology and due to this each gender adapted differing responses, in particular with this Natural Selection subcategory and as a result have remarkably differing responses within it; Hypergamy and Hypogamy. Initially I'll start with those traits both sexes select for and then take each gender individually in Part I (for women) and Part II (for men).

The most fundamental social Display dimorphism we can exhibit is the ability to acknowledge another person. To recognize that they exist and that we're sharing space and time with them, even in passing. It's referred to as a greeting, or colloquially, as saying "Hi". For some individuals hugging the tight end of the friend zone, just saying "hello" or "hi" to people will be anxiety laden. For others, it's a matter of a lacking the habit and as a consequence they never picked up on additional social skills that would have evolved from this initial greeting. This should be an obvious starting point: going out and learning to get into the habit of greeting and acknowledging people. Learn to hold eye contact and have a smile that doesn't look like you've just put on a mask or are imitating a chimpanzee in the act of submission. Learn to genuinely speak to the individuals around you as living, breathing human beings that have feelings and complexities of their own. Learn to be interested in them. Learn to express care and compassion that goes beyond reflexive social greetings. As an added bonus, get in the habit of saying goodbye as well. I make a habit of speaking to everyone who takes care of me. I greet them, ask how their day is going, genuinely smile, thank them and then say goodbye or wish them to have a good day. It's a social pattern; a social pattern that shows greater interest and sharing of values and is but a single step from a conversation.

In attempting to initiate a conversation with others, who we may only marginally know, if at all, we shouldn't be focused immediately into trying to hold a conversation from an outset, as neither party is truly invested in the other and may not be receptive to the overture. By utilizing lighthearted and teasing remarks that are meant to amuse, we can test the waters of receptivity and to demonstrate skill in social conventions. Banter should be fun, outgoing, with a positive energy base and strangely is often content free. Research banter lines for a good idea of the tremendous range and situational contexts it typically is utilized in. The goal is to establish a mood and frame for people to feel more relaxed and open to furthering social engagement. Having fun makes people feel good and lightens the mood, but the real key to banter is it establishes shared commonality (being social together) and that is the initiation for rapport that we're truly seeking.

There is a technique that combines branding, marketing and advertising into a socialized process. Somewhere someone coined it as Mayor Walking. It is the process of overtly being intentionally social with numerous groups of people to win social favor and to get people to like you. Most people who attempt this fall into the trap of trying to entertain, which is a mistake. The key is to make a series of short rapport building conversations and then bounce and come back later to continue (this reduces pressure, tension and seeds expectation). An advance version is very much like juggling multiple conversations. Our goal here is to be friendly, open and engaging with a number of people holding short and brief conversations. When we are, the people who find us engaging and attractive will let us know with their attention and time. Those who don't, we're not invested in and we've just been friendly. No harm, no foul. Their lack of interest is not something we have to beat ourselves up over and take so seriously. We simply move on to those that do find us engaging.

What is the essence of a social display dimorphism? How about holding an engaging social conversation? The ability to spark conversations that are dynamic, involved, that establish mutual rapport and emotional connections is an attractive trait valued by both men and women. In fact, the ability to develop personal connections and rapport with individuals is a prime non-physical attraction characteristic, even when viewed from afar and not actually partaken in (think of someone holding court in an engaging conversation). One so valued, that when we're inexperienced we can make the mistake of focusing overly on being interesting, captivating and entertaining when we're still at the level where we're just trying to hold a conversation with others. The biggest mistake novices make is trying to start a whole conversation, rather than leading with banter and transitioning to a conversation by showing interest where it is found/discovered/shared via the banter interaction.

Inexperienced individuals will go to lengths to memorize humorous stories, jokes or turns of phrases in order to seem wittier, smarter and more charming than they are. That can really help in the short run, but the problem is what happens when you run out of script, or the situation goes off context? You're screwed! I've seen it happen, really. It's sad. It's terrifying if you're the one going through it.

Almost as bad, is the individual who doesn't know what to say and reverts to trying to show interest, develop a connection and build rapport by asking interview type questions; "what do you do", "where do you work", "where you from", "how old are you", "how many siblings do you have" etc. It's god awful, because the answers don't lead to a conversation. The conversation doesn't open up and we don't really learn anything of real value about someone other than factual statistics.

Worst yet, it leads to people trying to relate to their own question in return. If they asked where someone worked then tried to "relate" by stating where they work, without being asked. If they asked, "where are you from", again they listen and then try to "relate" by telling the person where they're from too. This is painful. It not only demonstrates a lack of social conversation skills and ability to lead socially, but also demonstrates a neediness and desire to connect. People of social value don't do this. They don't have a need that requires filling; they're self-fulfilled in being social as they have the skills and experience of being social on a regular and sustained basis.

So how does someone who isn't fluent in social conversations engage in a conversation in a fluid way? How about not talking? Really. Stop trying to lead a conversation and be interesting. Ask a question, and instead of trying to "relate", be interesting by being "interested". Ask a follow up question relating to their answer; why's that? Tell me more about that, what's that mean to you, how does that make you feel, etc. Even if you ask the awful interview type questions, you can develop a measure of rapport and connection in finding the value behind the answer. This is the essence of developing a connection: understanding other people's values, experiences and perspectives. It's what makes people interesting.

If you asked, "how many siblings do you have" and they respond, following up with "what was that like for you", is far better than saying you have four brothers named Jason, Tim, Patrick and Chris. Try that on for size and if you have to write out the follow up questions, do so. Memorizing a short list of follow up questions is far better than trying to memorize a social script. But we can make it really simple; just start with one follow up question. That will put you ahead of most everyone else who doesn't. Can you imagine where you'd be socially if you could manage two follow up questions? Here's a short list;

- Why's that?
- Tell me about that.
- What was that like for you?
- How did that make you feel?
- What does that mean to you?

The MAP- A Personal Guide to the Sexual Marketplace

To close the conversation thread from going on and on, I'll thank them for sharing. I'll acknowledge the value they provided by being open, honest and vulnerable. When people are recognized, valued and appreciated for their actions you're likely to see more of those behaviors. If we are hoping to engage people in conversations, creating a safe and open place where they feel free to share and welcome really helps. At a fundamental level people want to be seen and recognized; we're mammals and as mammals we're social. It's in our DNA. We want to converse, we want to connect, we want to be seen and recognized. Our deep seeded emotional needs are being met and when our needs are met, and so we find those individuals who do this for us attractive. Later we will investigate how to transition from attraction to desire, but first we have to establish ourselves as attractive individuals socially.

Both sexes would also reap a harvest of benefits if they just stood up straight, stopped slouching and meekly walking or shuffling their feet as they walked. Individuals not confident in themselves don't occupy physical space with confidence and instead try to reduce their spatial volume and meekly walk ,if not trudge along as they move. Be willing to be seen. Carry yourself as though your worthy of being seen. When you do, you're telling others you have self-worth, self-respect and self-confidence. When you don't, you're sub communicating the opposite. When you're not confident and assured of yourself, why should others be? When you have confidence, you're going to be willing to take up personal space and this is an indication of having personal boundaries. When you don't have good personal boundaries, you're inviting a lack of respect for those boundaries. It's worth saying again; a failure to have appropriate boundaries is an invitation to others to violate those boundaries- something you're actively communicating via body language. How a person stands is an immediate non-verbal indicator of this because it is coupled with the inability to say "no". People who stand poorly have a difficult time saying "no" to others. Weak boundaries are an invitation for others to exploit you and how you stand communicates this. Ultimately when your combined behaviors are not self-interested, you can expect others to receive that signaling. An individual who won't serve their own self-interest won't serve the interests of others very well. If you can't take care of your business, how can I have any expectation that you'll take care of "our" business if we're partners?

Flipping to the other side of the exact same coin, recognizing that other people have personal boundaries and space is critically important to social acceptance. When we violate someone's sense of personal space, we are actively displaying a lack of social awareness and appropriateness, which is a form of disrespect, and whether we mean it or not, it will be perceived that way. The important concept here is to understand that minor signals of a lack of respect (such as violating an individual's personal space) are an early indication of failure to respect boundaries and people will make assumptions about your future behavior. This is a warning signal we receive. When repeated, people will naturally start to separate themselves from you both physically and socially. A key to resolving this is to mirror body spacing and body spacing behaviors. When someone is leaning or pulling away, give them physical space. Learning this can be terribly uncomfortable, kind of creepy and awkward too, but better that than the alternative. A refined adaptation to this skill is to try to work with spacing subtly. An appropriate analogy is dance; initially novice dancers are really stiff, the movements are deliberate and unrefined. With greater experience and mastery, the movements are unnoticeable and seem natural.

Even more difficult but equally relevant is a social familiarity with gestures and appropriate touch. The complexities here are both wide and deep and would be a great subject for further research if you have trouble with this element of socialization. Truth be told most people do. Even normal people get it wrong or make social faux pas from time to time. Again self-awareness, social context, practice and learning from past missteps are essential. There is a reason why in Toast Masters your first speech is simply an introduction. It is far more efficient to start at a basic level and concept and build up, than to fully critique and improve on a complex and encompassing performance. Same too for socialization and touch. Learning

The MAP- A Personal Guide to the Sexual Marketplace

the fundamental basics and getting confident in the skill and application of it is far better than an imagined tango of sensual seduction.

Part I Gender Differentiation Social Display Selection (for Women)

Because men and women faced significantly different environmental and social challenges due to mammalian sex differences, we responded evolutionarily to those challenges with differing adaptations. In terms of sexual selection, they are incredibly pronounced in the Natural Selection subcategory of Social Display Dimorphisms, i.e. masculinity and femininity. I'll start with the female social display traits associated with soliciting a Hypogamic response in men, because they are the most limiting on a biological and social level.

> Hypogamy: the male predilection for selection based on feminine social display traits associated with youth, fertility and variety.

Because males are not the gender faced with the biological challenge of internal fertilization, a prolonged gestation period and the task of nourishing the young, as well as the desire to know that his genes had the greatest possible chance of being passed to the next generation, a natural process of selecting for youth, fertility, and variety in women developed.

> Youth- While we cannot control our age and actual youth is limited, we do not have to become aged beyond our years and can still learn to express social displays that characterize youth. People exhibiting the biological markers of youth (vigorous, good health, physically beautiful) socially tend to be physically active, outgoing, curious, engaging, positive, supportive, adventurous, playful, energetic, etc. They're youthful. They act, behave and live in a vibrant way. They have an effervescent outlook on life. In selecting for a partner, we are also aware that social contagions exist; the emotional energy or frame from one person is transferable to another and is capable of

The MAP- A Personal Guide to the Sexual Marketplace

spreading like a virus. Having a youthful personality is a partnering plus, as negativity is demoralizing and destructive. Positivity, youthful exuberance and a sense of joy is something we will gravitate toward. It's something that we will gladly open our lives to and for.

Fertility- The most obvious selection criterion, fertility goes well beyond the willingness to reproduce, and deeply into variances sexually. Body symmetry, facial symmetry, particulars regarding preference in body and genitalia shape and proportions (lips, tits, abs, legs, ass etc) are all physical traits associated with fertility, and while we cannot control our genetics, how our physical traits are displayed socially is within our control.

> Please note; while plastic surgery is an option, body modification that emphasizes sexuality to overcome a deficiency in emotional and behavioral maturity (friend zone) is an invitation to a greater disaster and I absolutely do not recommend it if you are here. You're not friend zoned (men not wanting to have sex with you) because your tits are too small, your lips are too narrow, and you have a sloped flat ass. You're here because of your behavioral expressions and changing those will change your results without inviting bigger problems. Or let me put it a little more bluntly: putting lipstick on a pig doesn't change the nature of the pig. Furthermore, you're ill prepared to handle the social conditions associated with hyper sexuality, as you're failing already. If you're ill-prepared to handle a given tool, a larger, more complex tool isn't advisable.

With having said that, learning standard grooming, dress and cultural beauty practices are essential to normalized social behavior. Having clean, healthy hair and a hair style that fits your facial profile, personality style and life style will have an immediate impact, as will a wardrobe that equally reflects those same criteria. Let's also not forget the little things as they tend to be a great indicator to personality and charter composition; finger nails and toe nails. You can tell a lot about a woman by looking at her hands. Want to double check that assessment? Check out her feet. Nothing screams low class, low value and drama ridden like fucked up toe nails and whacked out toe nail polish (I'll probably say this a number of times, but crazy will reveal itself. It cannot be denied. It will not be denied. Everyone's job is to look for it, and once found, get rid of it.). Ladies watch those toenails, as good men know to look.

What is less obvious about the fertility sub classification is the emphasis placed on child rearing - traits associated with caring, nurturing and supportive nature. When we talk about social displays, does a woman's behavior indicate that she would make an appropriate maternal mate when we consider selecting for a partner and not just a romp? A massive part of human sexual mating success is the emphasis on child development. Species that don't have a far lower quality of offspring that fare far worse in terms of mortality and continued reproductive success. In terms of Natural Selection (as opposed to Social Selection) we are focused on a mothers competitive, assertive and aggressive nature to not only defend and provide for herself, but also for her child. These traits are initially seen in female intra-sexual competition for male mates. It is incredibly foolish and short-sighted to believe that the intra-species competition for mates (female vs. female) isn't as competitive as male-male competition. Dominant, assertive and aggressive females (Alpha Females) get choice pick in almost any subject that has been studied and observed, both socially and in natural environments. This is true for all mammal and social species. Want to increase your fertility selection viability? Learn to speak up for yourself, become assertive and learn to be aggressive enough to go after what you want and be willing to defend it from others (the result of this is social rank and standing). This is the emotional side of being physically seen. In this case, be willing to be emotionally seen. Be willing to emotionally take up space. Learn to express your feelings, communicate your expectations to others and have those expectations honored by others. Women who have poor emotional boundaries, make poor mothers and poor partners. While physical fertility may be out of your control, the social display traits clearly are not.

Variety - At its root is the male genetic desire for multiple sexual partners to diversify the gene pool, but variety also transcends beyond just sex.

(Note: Women are equally driven for genetic variety but manifest it differently. as Dr. Helen Fisher's research into naturally occurring human breeding cycles and divorce cycles show remarkable parallels with and fall neatly into the genetic mating strategy associated with serial monogamy and genetic diversification.)

If we're below the sexual threshold, it's pretty hard to talk about providing sexual variety to be selected based on this, but variety doesn't just mean sex. Variety is grouped in the "provisional dimorphisms" of Natural Selection. Here's a hint: human males are social mammals which indicates that bonds are formed via social care. If variety is valued, perhaps the variety can and should be provided in a provisional manner socially. Being supportive, nurturing, caring and an overall fan base for a man is an incredible asset when we're talking about a potential partner. Additionally, how about a partner in crime (figuratively), someone creative, outgoing and spontaneous, - these traits just might fit the bill of variety that men would be looking for in a potential partner. Instead of 'making plans' for the evening, how about suggesting that the two of you walk the town and find/discover someplace intriguing that you wouldn't have sought out in advance. Bonus points to the girl who can actually recommend something, rather than saying, "I don't know, what do you want to do?" Help us out. If you are able to help provide options or signal in advance of a place you'd like to try will go a long way in feeling that we have a 'partner' in the matter.

Part II Gender Differentiation Social Display Selection (for Men)

Hypergamy: the female predilection for selection based on masculine social display traits associated with social standing & rank, displays of wealth and power.

There are significant ramifications and manifestations associated with the social selection traits associated with a mammalian reproductive system, particularly for females. It would have been essential for females to sexually select a mate who could protect her and her child, possessed and commanded resource or the ability to acquire them and had a willingness to provide for her and her child, in addition to other social benefits acquired through this social pairing within the greater social group. Additionally, competitive male displays and acts of aggression and dominance are utilized to both attract mating partners and to also intimidate and scare off rivals in competition for females. Given this biological starting point it is entirely understandable that females would have selected males based on social displays associated with social standing and rank, wealth and power.

Social Standing and Rank: A man's standing and social rank is determined by the measure in which he has been found to be assertive, aggressive and dominant amongst his competitors and is the single most important subcategory, as these traits typically are precursors to the others. It is for this reason, applying more alpha traits of assertiveness, aggression and dominance socially will have the greatest impact upon a man's social worth and sexual market value. While this is remarkably, true a problem occurs when uncalibrated individuals attempt to role model individuals at the higher end of the spectrum without having a solid grasp of the fundamentals. The typical result is not increasing assertiveness, aggressiveness and dominance in a socially appropriate and acceptable way, but really laying on the asshole and douche bag behavior. That won't work. Keep in mind, if a man is in the friend zone, he is exhibiting below average levels in alpha traits, particularly due to low self-esteem. He won't speak up, he supplicates, and he has little ability to say no to a woman. His preference is to increase pro-social, pro-relationship behaviors (beta traits) which is not a sexual selection strategy. It is a relationship strategy. If those behaviors really worked he'd have little need for this book. He should save the beta behavior until he's in a relationship. The key point to this is that while women love beta traits, they simply are not turned on by them, and because of that he is being over-looked.

Displays of Wealth: Wealth is a profound indication of a male's ability to not only provide for himself and be independent, but to over-produce and to provide for a potential mate and their children. While personal net worth and spending habits are reasonable benchmarks and indications of wealth and resource acquisition, other factors play prominent roles in the selection evaluation process:

> Education- The value of an education to affect productivity, value and worth are well established (education to earnings), but less recognized are the socializing elements associated with leadership, management, team building and group cooperation that are a by-products of higher education that play out as valued traits in the sexual marketplace.

Occupation- Ones profession of work, trade or employment will give an early and direct indication as to the earning potential of a prospective mate, as well as the social signals of prestige and respect associated with and afforded to differing occupations. The choice of occupation will also be an indication of a man's willingness to sacrifice himself to achieve his earning potential in the choice of specific work. Occupations devoid of the requirement to sacrifice free time, vacation, safety, etc. tend to be socially valued less and held in lower esteem.

Mannerisms- How a man speaks and acts, from his diction to his annunciation all give indicators of social status, education and earning potential. From an evolutionary perspective, as social creatures, those that were able to conduct themselves well in the social pack or group stood the best chance of survival and reproduction. Mannerisms, etiquette and adherence to cultural norms demonstrate social allegiance and acceptance, and thus individuals can be identified as being members of the dominant social group or class.

Dress and grooming- If a picture is worth a thousand words, a first impression is a motion picture, and influences opinions accordingly. In this regard a man's sense of style, dress and grooming habits are his personal brand. It speaks to his attitude, confidence, emotional state and values. He should think of himself as a company. Is his brand something he'd really expect a woman to buy into? If not, that needs to change.

Social displays of power: Normally when discussing the Natural Selection traits associated with power and an ability to influence or control the behaviors of other people, we mean one's ability to hold sway, influence or convince others through physical presence or reputation. The problem is that for those men stuck in the friend zone, they haven't mastered themselves let alone learned the ability to hold sway over others. The most significant element a man can start to address here is his ability to exercise power and control over his own emotional energy when dealing with other people in the following manner:

Nervous energy as opposed to stable energy- A surefire indication of someone's social status is their typical energy state; people of low status and low self-esteem tend to be uncomfortable, needy and anxious and their behaviors reflect this. These insecure behaviors telegraph a lack of control, influence and power, which is the antithesis of behaviors reflected in high status and powerful people.

Restless movements as opposed to relaxed & smooth – A nervous or anxious individual will have rapid, short and uneasy movements when they speak or interact with others due to the manifestation of and release of this nervous energy they don't have command over, whereas someone in command of himself and his environment will move in an almost delayed and graceful manner, as if they were moving under water.

Contractive body language as opposed to expansive and open body language-
When someone feels threatened or insecure their body language tends to be defensive and protective, their arms huddling around themselves and rarely if ever do their gestures break the outside plane of their silhouette. High value and status individuals on the other hand tend to stand, present and gesture in bold, broad and open movements.

An important concept to become familiarized with is that people of status have already achieved that status and therefore are not in the habit of trying to obtain it. They already manifest those traits. When we are attempting new skills often it is going to be terribly rough and discombobulated in execution. While there is great value in learning and attempting new things, we should be hesitant in continually faking it. Power, status and social control is very much like a Chinese Finger Puzzle, the more we force it the more counterproductive it is.

Sexual Display Dimorphisms- The single most feared and titillating subject we'll cover and is relevant to both sexes: the realm of human sexual display, enticement, provocation and execution. It is also a subject that most people have little experience in, let alone received any meaningful instruction, coaching or mentoring. If they had, we wouldn't be here. Nature would just take care of itself. Sexual displays are not all that complicated when broken down and like any skill, studied and practiced. Most people are not competent with these concepts and therefore lack confidence in all of them. It doesn't help when they are so central to our sense of personal masculinity and femininity that when we have a misstep, are rejected or our hopes dashed, that we over emphasize the experience in a negative way. With all of that in mind, we are going to slow down, take it one step at a time, identify the fundamental elements, and provide actionable behaviors you can work and practice on in a set sequence:

Sexual Display: Previously we've indicated rather directly that you don't exhibit nor spark physical attention, interest or arousal let alone sexual arousal and self-regard. A refined sexual display in a man goes beyond walking with a pronounced swagger. An outstanding example would be how Robin Thicke walks onto the stage following a much younger and sexually conspicuous Miley Cyrus at the 2013 VMA Awards (truly go watch it). The sheer number of micro expressions exhibited within seconds tell a very compelling, clear and convincing narrative of who his is and how he is to be regarded. It's the swagger in his walk, the large arm-swing held in contrast to his casual hand in his pocket, to his not only upright posture, but how he's there to 'see and be seen' unflinchingly and unashamed or embarrassed. The clothing and accessories just further telegraph his 'bad-boy' persona. An intermediate sexual display would be the same mannerism, just toned down and less pronounced. The same for the clothing and accessories. A basic level would be walking confidently, with good upright posture. Sexual display is all those elements combined with a sensualized expression in dress, manner and behavior. Focusing primarily on physical and social confidence will do marvels here (so much so they have their own specific sexual selection category) and adding a touch of sensuality in dress, manner and behavior is all the spice you really need to change a given dish (you). Wearing a skin tight, uncomfortable dress that barely covers your hooch, or for guys opening your shirt to your navel isn't what we should be doing here. Neither will aping similar traits of over sexualized manners and behaviors (don't actually mimic or replicate being Robin Thicke). It won't work for you because it isn't you. You don't have the social skills, confidence and social awareness to pull it off, not yet at least. Stick with the fundamentals; physically carry yourself with confidence, dress confidently, act with certainty, be engaging, open and connect with people by having playful banter and engaging conversations. The more people you connect with the more attractive socially and sexually you'll become. Remember highly social people tend to be social leaders. Leaders are considered "alpha" by nature. By becoming highly social, you're shifting your position within society toward its locus of power, even if you don't carry the trapping or cultural symbols of it. For social creatures, being social is a prerequisite, excelling at it makes you a social leader.

Note: The following, while encompassing significant elements of sexual displays independently, they are also presented in the overall general order of progression process.

> Body Language: Sexual display also involves the nonverbal behavioral communication practices that signal intentions, feelings, thoughts and receptivity to sexual advances, through facial expression, body positioning and gestures that have culturally codified meaning. A tremendous amount of information is revealed through social behaviors if we're willing to observe it and to spend the time to effectively interpret it. Just as though we've learned that laughing and smiling are indicators of happiness, approval and acceptance, prior to someone stating so verbally, we need to recognize that social sexual behaviors of interest, acceptance and approval are initially communicated non-verbally as well. These non-verbal displays are referred to as Indicators of Interest (IOIs) and initial IOIs are geared toward creating social openings and invitations. Often these indicators are unconsciously presented or can be broadly interpreted, thus leading to immense amount of confusion or doubt, so study, observation and even practice are paramount. There is just no substitute for seeing and observing complex human interactions such as these in their various sexual phases and in real time. As the sexual phases progress, the indicators of interests, increase in intensity (becoming more overt), direction (becoming more sexual) and focus (toward a specific individual).

Sexual Enticement: A distinct shift from base physical and social attraction to arousal. It utilizes IOIs, light flirting and social touching to inject an interaction with a sexual tone and to evaluate receptivity toward further advancement.

<u>Directed Indicators of Interest (IOIs):IOIs:</u> Body language or mannerisms that convey a specific interest toward a single individual and signals receptivity to engaging socially with that individual. Put simply, they are behavioral signals of attraction. The list of IOIs is endless, but on a basic level they will include elements associated with the desire to be close and available. You will hold the individual's attention and their body posture will more directly face yours over time. There will be concerns toward appearance manifested in self-grooming and self-caressing to reassure themselves, such as reflexively touching and stroking of her hair or subtle straightening of her clothes and appearance. Their mannerisms will start to synchronize with yours to unconsciously build connection and unity in mirroring posture, gestures and energy levels. There will be prolonged eye contact, intensity coupled with conscious shyness and averting of gaze matching. They will continue to build rapport by carrying on a conversation thread by showing increased interest or mutual sharing, often reinitiating conversation when a lull is presented. These are by no means an exhaustive representation of the myriad of expressive gestures that convey interest or attraction, but the best way to realize how these are conveyed is to observe people engaging in them. Finding appropriate social venues where you can observe people interacting in a social-sexual manner is an invaluable asset to learning, understanding and recognizing them.

<u>Light flirting</u>: A social attempt to overtly amuse in order to win social favor and to suggest sexual interest and availability in a verbal manner. As a form of communication, it is meant to be playful and enjoyable by all those involved. Flirtation can take the form of expressing irony, wit, charm and employ the use of double entendre.

The MAP- A Personal Guide to the Sexual Marketplace

Frequently it will include elements of intentionally increasing tension and then releasing it in a "push-pull" fashion. The dynamics tend to be fairly simple; say something considered "mean" playfully then dovetail that with saying something nice or a reversed process of that. It is a combination of showing interest and being disinterested. Flirting commonly employs the techniques of shared and knowing glances to sub communicate intent, feelings or attitudes. Despite the fact that flirting takes a sexual nature it is not a sexual overture but utilized to initiate a sexual under current and to measure whether or not sexual advances will be accepted.

Social touching: sends powerful signals in social interaction, much like punctuation helps organize content and makes meaning more clear by emphasizing specific points. It should be done smoothly and confidently, as a natural and normal part of your self-expression. Social touching should be welcoming, comforting and relaxing- a way to defuse social and sexual tension by giving an outlet to those energies via physical expressions of mutual connectedness. A general failure to learn to communicate non-verbally through touching in a social-sexual environment creates an enormous gulf socially. The inability to touch properly in social situations is a severe handicap. In a social sense, you are a developmentally disabled mute.

Learning and developing these behaviors is going to be terribly challenging, especially so where you are highly conscious of it and these mannerisms are foreign to you. Focus on touching gestures that are casual and incidental, points of engagement where to emotionally connect with the individual or to emphasize a point in a conversation. This typically involves gestures that initiate physical contact and usually a quick or immediate withdrawal. They are momentary and fleeting.

Be aware of a person's emotional feedback in their behavioral micro-expressions: pulling away, a flinch or general body tension and overt discomfort. Reservation is a signal you've reached a personal boundary or comfort level. Respect boundaries. Pull away in proportion to the reaction to provide social and emotional refuge for them to regain their comfort and confidence in the social interaction. Should they change their mind, they'll signal such through additional indicators of interests or initiate the social contact themselves. We should respond in kind if we're open and receptive as well.

Sexual Provocation: Sexual provocation is about advancing the sexual frame and fanning the flames of desire and arousal by direct flirting, overt indicators of interest (IOIs), and intimate physical contact. The essence of sexual provocation is an overt display toward sexual interest to initiate reciprocal sexual behavior. Nothing subtle. Any gesture here is provocative by nature; " I'm having sexual thoughts, and I'm looking right at you.", and measuring their receptivity to these advances.

***If there has been no banter or flirting, do not skip the previous step. If someone isn't comfortable holding light, flirty banter with you, they're highly likely not to respond positively toward overt displays of sexual interest. Once we're more skilled in the Natural Selection traits can we realize those individuals with whom we can skip the sexual progression steps appropriately.

Direct Flirting: This is adult teasing and flirting. It is capitalizing on established social attraction, rapport and connection and transitioning into the sexual realm. It says, "I see you and I appreciate you as a sexual being." It should be playful and subtly sexual – because, after all, we are sexual beings. Sexualized banter isn't a come on, it isn't a fuck proposition, it's playfully teasing and engaging another human being in recognizing your mutual sexuality and bringing it to the forefront. This can be done regardless of adult age ranges, body image, social standing or status. This doesn't mean we whistle at strangers on the street, or aggressively sexualize strangers; this is playful banter with people with whom we have some established rapport. People who have already accepted us, and us them. It should be sexual in nature, implying or referencing your partner's attractiveness, desirability and your recognized interest in them. It should also be coupled with a measure of playful take away to build sexual tension and then release it often through playful rejection.

Keep in mind these are not fuck propositions, but they are a very real way to increase chemistry and to take a temperature reading. Are we at the boiling point or not? We're testing how they feel and how we're received. This is still technically at the teasing, tempting, bantering stage. We're still trying to figure out if this is someone we really want to take home and roll around with. The stakes are high all the way around, but it should be getting heated.

Overt Indicators of Sexual Interest (IOIs): While I think it is pretty obvious when someone openly states that they like and desire you in a sexual manner, what isn't (and are far more likely to be expressed) are the non-verbal overt indicators of sexual interest that are communicating the same thing. What we should be looking for is that moment in time where our social interaction transitions into a series of escalating and repeated layering of multiple direct indicators of interest being given simultaneously. This patterning of behavior should be mutually reciprocated, fueling the process of heightened attraction, attachment and arousal. That is, we recognize the signaling, accept it for what it is and respond back in kind.

At a progressive stage an individual will start to work the social logistics of staying in contact; they'll inquire about your plans, schedule and who'll you'll be doing that with. They may mention events and activities that you might be interested in joining them for. They'll exchange direct contact information and make plans to be with you. They will be openly choose you and your company over other options presented.

Intimate Physical Social Contact: As our comfort and confidence level increases with our physical displays of connection, there is an increased desire to sustain and maintain that physical contact that transitions into intimate personal contact. A simple way to increase physical contact is to slow down the motions and gestures, and to prolong or maintain the physical contact itself. We transition from a touch, to touching. From a caress, to a hold. From an individual gesture, to reciprocating gestures.

We're touching and having sexual thoughts and sharing those, all the while knowing it is welcome and desired. This doesn't necessarily mean direct genital stimulation, more typically it is simply physical contact in a socially appropriate and accepted way. Touching each other back and forth as we talk, reaching out and making contact while we talk, holding hands, playing finger caressing games, etc. Our bodies, legs, arms, feet are touching, not because there isn't room, but because we both want to be in contact.

The oven is hot and now we're cooking. We're either going to embrace the heat or we're going to GTFO of the kitchen. This goes for both parties. Either of us can end the interaction for any reason at any point. It's called safety. Be prepared, recognize it for what it is and be prepared to cool things off, just as before. It's the graceful and responsible thing to do (at this point it's also the fucking law!). While this can feel like a rejection, either of us can again change our minds at a later time.

The real problem with rejection isn't the rejection itself, but the associated feelings that come with it. A key to responding to rejection in a healthy way is to realize you're going to have a biological reaction. You're entitled to feel any way you want; however, you are not entitled to react any way you want. Being violent and abusive isn't just inappropriate and counter beneficial, but also against our civil laws governing behavior. One in which you'll be sure to lose.

It is important, therefore, to anticipate and understand your fundamental biological responses and how to counter them as they occur or present themselves. When you get rejected you're engaged in a limbic response; it's all fight or flight - not a great place for rational thought. Our first step is to get the hell out of limbic response thinking and reacting. A deep, calming breath can work wonders. It may take more than one or two. That's fine. Do it. In our biological evolution, we developed this massive cerebral cortex, as a process of environmental and social adaptation to challenges greater than simple rejection. Capitalize on that rich inheritance and insist that you utilize it. Realize that you're having a number of hormonal and biological responses geared directly toward you to mate and to focus on a single individual to achieve those aims; at this point whoever you're currently fixated on. You're fighting biology here, not just having an emotional response to a rejection. It's going to be hard, really hard, but necessary. Keep in mind the big picture: you were able to advance a relationship to the rejection point. You can repeat that process if you are aware of the skills, attributes and traits associated with that process. It can be replicated again, and opportunity is the greatest of salves. We feel rejection strongest where we have the most at stake or feel we have no other recourse or options. I can empathize and sympathize with the first, the second we can do something about together.

The emphasis of all this is to play socially and physically but play nicely. Sexual escalation, while a contact sport, shouldn't be competitive. It's not win/lose. It's an inclusive social process and others should want to be social, to be sexual and to play with us because of the environment in which we create for those events to occur within.

Sexual Execution: Sexual escalation is rarely a linear process - it just won't happen in an A, B, C fashion. If you want assurances your advances are welcomed, you need to take each step slowly and to make sure you have consent throughout each phase. If not, we are going to have to reclaim lost or ceded ground. Honestly, early on it's going to be pretty bad. No Rico Sauvé here. It's a lot like learning to drive a manual car: starts, stops, grinding of the gears, stalls and terribly unsmooth actions. But don't let that stop you. It's a learning process. Everyone goes through this. In time, practice and dedication it becomes a secondary reflex that allows you to actually enjoy the scenery and journey as you mindlessly shift gears and motor on.

Until then, any hesitancy here by either party should be recognized. Fears, misunderstandings, misconceptions, whatever the issue is, it needs to be discussed and resolved if we're to proceed. There is a tremendous difference between jitters of anticipation and someone who's in over their head. Everyone needs to be able to freely say "no" and put everything on pause. Why? Because the shit gets very, very real from this point out. Everyone at this point recognizes the importance of a condom for sexual protection. Sexual consent is legal protection. If you don't have open and freely given consent, everything is an all stops. Sex is a no go until full and unmitigated consent is expressly given. You just don't go forward, ever without consent. Ladies, this is a really good time to get really graphic about your desires and wishes. Make it so obvious, you'd be ashamed to say the same thing in front of a jury. Guys you'd better be prepared to ask for just that, too. That btw, won't be a deal killer. Most guys actually find that rather hot. For example, I try to get my girlfriend to talk dirty to me in public all the time, but thats our thing. Feel free to make it your own.

With all that being said, there is a massive difference between "not now" and "no". No, means no! I don't believe in safe words. For your safety AND MINE, I'll insist upon it. But there are times when "not now" really is an invitation to try again in a differing manner. My clearest example of this was the greatest Pick Up Artist I have ever known; Handsome, my bulldog. He was incredible. He had a knack for seeing who to approach and had no reservations in doing so and making himself known. He had no shame in singling out the individual he was interested in pursuing and then sequestering them for private time. Actually, private time was really a special time bubble the two of them created, as everyone was still in the room. It was all in his body language. He would reach out with a paw, touch the individual and they would either comply by petting him or not. If they did, it was on. If not, he didn't take it personally. He just recalibrated and reached out again. Rejected twice, he'd take a completely different approach, typically even a very physical change in position from one side to another. He would actually elicit a change in mood to promote a change in results. That was an OMG moment for me - get the individual to laugh and have fun and then see if the same proposition just presented is still no. If no was still no, he reverted back to where he was on solid ground by having fun, relaxing and exploring other options. What I found amazing was how often at that point the individuals who rejected him sought HIM out. The really crazy thing is that he would play one interested party off of another. It was shameless. It was also completely within his reality. He was just this really cool dude people wanted to spend time with, and he wasn't worried if it was one, two or three. He also had no shame regarding his sexuality and expressing desire for it. It was really awesome to watch. Stunning really. I learned a lot. I also, when the time came, told my English Bulldog to get off of the couch and leave my guest alone. Whether it's Handsome my English Bulldog, or Henry Ford quoted as saying "If you think you can or you can't, you're right!" your mind set is vastly more important than anything you bring to a situation. The lessons are the same from both: confidence and certainty. Never leave home without them and if you're ever in a situation where you want to change your partners mind, try changing their mood, rather than asking again with the same approach.

At a fundamental and basic level one of the of biggest challenges we face is the first kiss. There's so much pressure and we will always fear being rejected. This fear drives hesitancy and hesitancy is an active display of a lack of confidence and certainty which isn't attractive. There's a Bushido quote that says, "hesitancy killed the samurai." You should be able to recognize when sexual tension is high and kiss your partner then, when you're both in the moment or you lose attraction value by vacillating. Waiting is a fool's mistake because it leads to greater hesitancy, lack of confidence, increased uncertainty, loss of attraction value, sexual energy and ultimately a lost moment.

We also need to take the first kiss truly into context. Aa kiss is not a contract, but it is very nice." (Shout out there to the Novelty band Flight of Conchords.) If we make our first kiss simple, sweet and nice, it leaves room for something more and it takes some of the pressure off. Go slow, be gentle and don't make it into a grand testament to your worth or value. Even if you get rejected; you can still ask, "no, or not now?" playfully. It shows commitment and confidence. At least you will have made the attempt. There's something to be said about missing 100% of the shots you don't take.

Here's a problem with first kisses: they tend to be kind of not great. It's almost to be expected. The key is to lower your expectations and have a game plan for this eventuality. I personally like to acknowledge this and grade it (with great humor) and steeply curve it on the down side (most don't get beyond a 8th grade rating), "well that was quite nice... it reminds me of Margery, my 6th grade crush. She kissed like that... rather nice actually.... Rather sweet.... My mother would approve." The key to all this is to keep it light and fun. Of course, I offer a follow up. All of this is nothing more than bait for a follow up. Make sure it's seen that way. A mediocre first kiss can then be turned into a series of increasingly better kisses, with the cumulative effect of a great first kiss experience, which is what we all want.

It is incredibly important to remember sexual contact is the genetic glue that binds people together. We are simply hardwired biologically to respond to sexuality. When we don't execute on the

The MAP- A Personal Guide to the Sexual Marketplace

first kiss, we miss out on leveraging this natural biological response system. Biology and nature really are in our corner here and help ensure you get the full biological impact. Make the kiss last for more than a quick fast moment in time. Less than that and the limbic reward centers of the brain doesn't kick in. The kiss should be gentle, smooth, and slow with a lingering effect which then creates a biological "boom"!

All this then begs another quandary; when do you follow up a first kiss? A simple answer is "Strike while the iron is hot!". There's no better time for a second kiss than following a first one. There are several benefits for doing so. First, who wants to stop with a single kiss? Second it develops confidence and familiarity, which reduces hesitancy. It also sets everything up for a third kiss...

In light of everything I've just written and you've read, we're talking about a tremendous amount of material. A tremendous amount of material that you are most likely unfamiliar with and lies beyond your sense of comfort, security and mastery. That's OK. The reality is that it generally takes years if not a life-time to get average with all this by taking small and singular actions to improve with the corresponding results that are seemingly less grand than the efforts put forth. The importance of that then is that small, simple and basic steps are not going to get you the results you most likely want. You're going to need to take substantial action and leave your sense of security and comfort behind to transform. And you'll need to do so on a regular basis. This is the social equivalent of working out; you're going to have to lift heavy and regularly over a sustained training period. Worse yet, if you're in the friend zone, in order to get to average you're going to have to cross the 'creepy' zone. Your initial efforts are not necessarily going to be well received and that is going to sting. No doubt. It will get you down and defeat you if you let it. Notice those reactions for what they are. Prepare emotionally for those. Don't talk yourself down, but up. Take the small steps and in even graduations. Take notes, start a journal, reflect on both of those. Write out your successes. Reflect on those each time you journal, have a moment of pause for when you're getting down. Write down short, medium and yearlong goals. Track those. Develop plans and execute on those plans to achieve short and medium goals. Make sure your short-term goals lead up to your medium goals and your medium goals lead up to your yearlong goals. Ultimately have confidence and certainty with yourself that you're not only capable but worthy of being the individual you would like to become; because each of us are.

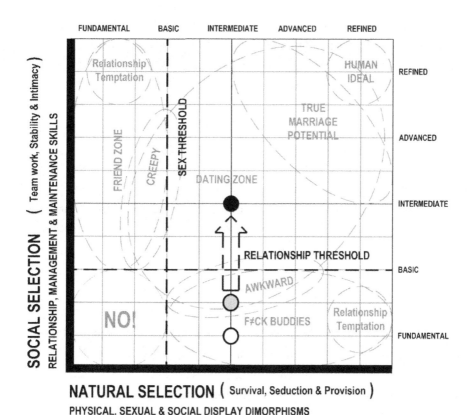

FUNDAMENTAL   BASIC   INTERMEDIATE   ADVANCED   REFINED

SOCIAL SELECTION (Team work, Stability & Intimacy)
RELATIONSHIP, MANAGEMENT & MAINTENANCE SKILLS

Relationship Temptation

HUMAN IDEAL — REFINED

TRUE MARRIAGE POTENTIAL — ADVANCED

FRIEND ZONE

CREEPY

SEX THRESHOLD

DATING ZONE — INTERMEDIATE

RELATIONSHIP THRESHOLD — BASIC

AWKWARD

NO!

F#CK BUDDIES

Relationship Temptation — FUNDAMENTAL

NATURAL SELECTION (Survival, Seduction & Provision)
PHYSICAL, SEXUAL & SOCIAL DISPLAY DIMORPHISMS

Fuck Buddies

If you are here (Fuck Buddy Zone), relative to your Social Selection traits you command a disproportionate level of biological and socially innate Natural Selection traits and attributes associated with physical beauty, social charm and influence while exhibiting a strong command of sexual enticement, arousal and sexual talent. Unfortunately, emphasis of Natural Selection traits is not a relationship strategy, they are a mating and sexual strategy. These strengths do not promote, sustain and maintain relationships. They are geared toward creating and stimulating sexual arousal and attention, which may lead to the desire for a relationship, but these are not the traits involved in fostering and supporting relationships successfully long term. When attraction and arousal interests wane within a sexual based relationship, so goes the relationship. As such, your relationship life is devoid of any meaningful stable, long-term, and fulfilling relationships, because your skill sets are overly based on Natural Selection traits and attributes and you are weak in the Social Selection traits; those abilities which promote, sustain and maintain a relationship. While you may be desirable, pursued and have had a series of relationships, they are anything but stable, lasting or gratifying beyond the attraction phase of a new courtship. You can do this for partner after partner after partner, failed relationship after failed relationship, without ever truly considering the single constant variable that links all of them together; you! You're at the center of your relationships. You have control of the people you pursue and let into your life. Only you have control of your behaviors, as you navigate and manage your relationships. We can only blame circumstances and others, for the failures until we're forced to come to the realization that your results speak for themselves. If you had the ability to do better you would have, but you haven't because you can't. Wanting to be in a position to better guide a relationship is not the same thing as being in a position to guide a relationship. The really scary thing is we will never really know our abilities until they are actually tried. That's the importance of practice. Without a doubt you're going to be aware of the fundamental skills associated with relationships, their management and maintenance, but you're not adept at them when you actually need them. Let's be honest, these skills we're talking about are not difficult; what's difficult is the circumstances and situations in which you'll be engaged in having not mastered them. They are going to be highly stressful, full of tension and in conjunction with all this you're going to have to break old patterns of behavior. These things will be difficult. They are challenging and they do require you to move from your comfort zone in order to learn and grow. People don't naturally grow in their comfort zone. It is when we are challenged and move in a direction to try new things that we grow. By not having learned, developed or prepared yourself to truly have the relationship you need or want, you've set your course for relationship

The MAP- A Personal Guide to the Sexual Marketplace

failure. What you're doing isn't working and if you want things to change, you have to be the instrument of that change. Waiting for change to happen on its own is stuff of fairytales, only meant to appease children and succor irrational adults.

The most obvious starting point is to look at root sources of your conflicts and relationship failures. Each conflict within a relationship is signaling a tension between values within it. Each relationship failure points directly toward a structural fault that led to its ultimate collapse. Despite all of these pleas for help, attention and redress, you've avoided the yeoman's work of resolving them, modifying behavior or choosing better options (partners) to prevent them in the first place. It's far easier to cry over a loss and wash, rinse and repeat with someone new that you hope will be better. But it isn't getting easier. Or better. You're all cried out and the difficulties with washing and rinsing and starting over with someone new get ever more challenging, not only with each passing year, but as we each get less and less viably desirable. Nature coupled with time is rarely kind. What is even more unkind is not the passing of your beauty, but the reality that you've squandering it by not learning and acting upon not only on the lessons from your past, but from developing in maturity as a functional adult. Because of this, you're in no position to have anything but similar and continuing results of failed relationships until that point in time that even the continuation of the pattern is no longer sustainable.

Your relationships are in all likelihood subject to failure due to the a combination of following low levels of social selection traits, attributes and abilities from you and your selected partner:

- **Team Work**- The social ability and skills associated with team building beyond the lure of sexual attraction, power and fame. At a fundamental level you're failing to self-regulate and to screen and filter for an appropriate relationship partner. You ignore their overt warning signs and succumb only to your sexual impulses or desire for social power, influence and validation. You and your selected partner both lack practiced and honed interpersonal skills of

The MAP- A Personal Guide to the Sexual Marketplace

empathy that are associated with reducing tension, anxiety and conflict within a relationship and you both have failed at establishing critical lines of communication prior to needing them in times of strife or disagreement and thus have nothing to rely on when you really need it.

- **Relationship Stability**- Both you and your partner will have inadequate management abilities when it comes to regulating and controlling common relationship interactions of unspoken expectations, trust and respect. Because of this, you are not adept in utilizing relationship friction points that unfold within relationships (which is the stuff of life) to develop a conscious, shared understanding of your partner's needs or boundaries and grow together as a couple because of it. Instead you both lack impulse control and become defensive and aggressive, responding in a fight or flight mode to the detriment of all your relationships.

- **Intimacy**- The hormonal afterglow associated with a solid orgasm and great sexual experience is but one measure for creating intimacy. It is one that is deeply rooted in our biological DNA to compel us to mate and replicate, which is why it feels *so right*. The error is understanding that this naturally occurring genetic mating strategy is nothing but a short-term solution, to which there is no long-term solution outside of meeting and fulfilling other deeply seated needs of intimacy. These intimacy needs are associated with stability and longevity, maintaining relationship quality, positive relationship states and balancing the dialectic tensions (naturally opposing values) such as connectedness vs autonomy, predictability vs novelty etc. within a relationship.

Nobody likes seeing their weaknesses exposed and thrust into the forefront of their lives. Nobody. In the previous section, The Friend Zone, I stated that we cannot resolve that which we do not acknowledge. I actually doubt that you don't already know this or that you're unaware of the reasons for your failed relationships. I think you know. You know, because you've had a visceral reaction to what I was writing, as you saw yourself reflected in those descriptions. I'm having to tell you these things because you either don't have friends who are telling you (you've probably driven away the ones who would have, anyway) or you fail to actually listen to the messages being delivered because they aren't within your sense of reality. Either way, you don't have the support group you really need to see what you're missing and that places you at a terrible disadvantage. You're both blind and resisting reality. That is an excellent recipe for sustained misery. Misery that you're in control of. Misery you don't have to face, experience or sustain any longer if you would just stop resisting the message it is trying to convey to you.

Everyone is born with the capacity and innate desire to belong and to love. It's part of our rich mammalian genetic heritage. We're pre-programmed for it. It's completely natural and should be expected. The problem arises when that natural and native propensity is not provided or enabled, deficiencies arise. These manifests themselves in an inability to be at home emotionally, psychologically and physically with ourselves first and secondly with others, and later on, with our own children. Our emotional, psychological and behavioral maturation is stymied. We simply fail to mature through the developmental stages as we are supposed to and ultimately become prisoners, as adults, to that which we fail to confront.

Individuals at the Fundamental Level of Social Selection:

For those individuals at the fundamental level (bottom 20 percentile range) there have been a number of crucial factors that have led up to your present state of not acquiring, comprehending and utilizing social skill sets appropriately. In simple terms, you are way below the relationship threshold and for good cause. I have little doubt that the environment you were brought up in, parental make-up and childhood experiences adversely affected your development significantly. This is truly a human tragedy. I wish it wasn't the case, but ignoring it doesn't serve us and hasn't served you. We cannot change the past, but we can make ourselves aware of the why and what that lead to our current existence and how those experiences are manifesting themselves today. Part of the scope of this book is to help

The MAP- A Personal Guide to the Sexual Marketplace

you first recognize this reality and then to help you realize its importance. Later, you'll be better equipped to seek out an appropriate manner of resolving these issues and developing beyond them.

Individuals located in the fundamental level of Social Selection will manifest both the following fundamental elements of psychological development AND the basic elements of psychological development in the following section combined. If you fall within the fundamental level of Social Selection, make sure to read and apply both of these sections. Start with the fundamental level then work toward the basic. It should be particularly noted that all of the psychological development stages you should have gone through but did not (fundamental level) are a result of failures, neglect and outright abuse of those directly responsible for your care and wellbeing, not your own. As a result, you have been detrimentally harmed and aggrieved, and it is now adversely affecting you and your ability to live out a fulfilling and healthy existence. While this all may be true, your life is your own. You need to own it. Part of that is resolving those developmental issues and taking agency of your life moving forward.

Erik Erikson was an early psychologist and psychoanalyst renowned for his work on theories of psychological development, particularly in children and the specific role in which their environment played a central role in providing the context for the child's development and growth into a functional adult.

His first three developmental stages from infancy to approximately six years old are critical and in large part have to do with sour physical and emotional needs being consistently met, the development of our identity regarding sense of shame and embarrassment and our development of reasoning and morality associated with social behaviors. A failure to provide for these essential child development needs and requirements frequently leads to substantial development failures of the individual resulting in gross negative behavioral patterns. The greater the failure and trauma, the greater subsequent damage to the individual, which regularly results in actual neurological changes of the individual. Simply put, neglect, abuse and trauma directly impair normal brain development, in addition to the direct harm received through abuse and maltreatment.

Individuals who have been victimized by this level of maltreatment commonly develop antisocial personality disorders and a propensity for addiction to varying degrees. While the degree of sociopathy will vary, it is common for individuals to exhibit the following characteristics:

- Callous indifferent concern for the feelings of others.

- Gross and persistent attitude of irresponsibility and disregard for social norms, obligations and laws resulting in criminality.

- Systemic deception associated with lying and conning of others.

- Incapacity to maintain enduring relationships.

- Very low tolerance to frustration, with a low threshold for discharge of aggression and violence.

- Inability to learn from experience, particularly punishment.

- Markedly prone to blame others and society.

- Prone to impulsivity and emotional inclinations.

- Reckless disregard for the safety and wellbeing of others.

- Incapacity to experience guilt, shame or remorse through indifference or moral rationalization.

Even if your issues and subsequent developmental impairments cannot be fully resolved, they can be contained (outside of incarceration or suicide). At least, we can limit the damage and subsequent harm that you cause for yourself, as well as to others. Each of us don't start out at the same place in life and therefore, our journeys are not the same and cannot be measured by the same markers. We can however, be measured by our achievements, especially if those are stopping evil, abuse, neglect and subsequent human

The MAP- A Personal Guide to the Sexual Marketplace

trauma from propagating. In doing so, we have achieved a remarkable thing and should be rightfully proud.

If you identify with this type of personality and still care to seek answers, there's hope, it means that there is a moral conscious with motivation that can see the costs associated with antisocial behaviors. We know that for people who have been traumatized it is very difficult for them to be rational about that which they were traumatized by, whether childhood experiences, social and economic environmental context, or particular issues associated with personal development. This is why it is important to have a trained, objective and skilled practitioner help identify the sources of your self-concept, what trauma or detrimental experiences you may have experienced and to then assist you in rationally navigating these personal challenges appropriately. While connecting emotionally with personal tragedy and grief associated with trauma is therapeutic, there is a myth that once faced, trauma heals itself in time. Unfortunately coming to terms with trauma is only the beginning. Therapy is what comes after you've discovered the trauma. It is working your way through it, formulating better ways in which to move forward in a more grounded basis of self-concept and self-identity. It helps you create more appropriate behavioral patterns and practice utilizing those until you're self-sufficient and free from the behaviors that jeopardize your and others' lives.

While we have been focusing on the manifestations associated with acute abuse and physical neglect, it should be noted that emotional neglect is the most prevalent form of child abuse, accounting for more than half of all reported cases to child protection services. And while emotional neglect may be one of the least traumatic experiences adversely affecting children when compared to sexual abuse and physical violence, it does fail to provide a child with a real sense and experience of love, affection, security and emotional support that they will need in order to develop properly. Much of what science has come to understand about co-dependency, addiction and attachment disorders originate with emotional neglect that has been unresolved in development of the individual as an adult, which then manifests itself when we seek out relationship partners.

Individuals at the Basic Level of Social Selection:

For those individuals at the Basic Level of Social Selection criteria (20-40 percentile range) you too have several crucial factors that have led up to your present state of not acquiring, comprehending and utilizing interpersonal social skills appropriately. You are below the relationship threshold because your social skills are below average, which directly affects your results beyond your command of physical attraction, power, sexual promiscuity and fame. In other terms you're socially awkward or offensive and you lack social empathy and interpersonal skills appropriate for sustaining relationships.

In the earlier section on the Fundamental Level of Social Selection I introduced the work of Erik Erikson, an early psychologist and psychoanalyst known for identifying the psychological development stages of individuals. Where an individual is deficient at fulfilling these developmental patterns, they suffer from corresponding social maladjustments. Individuals at the Basic level suffer from insufficient or impaired development in what Erikson defined as the fourth stage (Industry vs. Inferiority) and fifth stages (Identity vs. Role Confusion) of personal development, between school age through adolescence.

Erikson's fourth development (Industry vs. Inferiority) is between 6-12 years of age, which is where we start to expand our social environment from immediate family and localized neighborhood friends to a much larger and more diverse social environment, with a transition of authority from parents to other figures, such as teachers and opinions of peer groups at school. Our experiences at school coupled with the opinions our peer groups are significant sources for our emerging sense of self concept and self-esteem. This is the environment in which we develop a sense or need to win approval, to demonstrate our individual competencies and a sense of pride in accomplishing them or finding humility in our failures (Industry). It is also the source of where we may start to feel inferior and develop doubts with ourselves in relation to the successes of our peers and expectations from others that we will take with us as we age, telling us our place within society.

While academic and athletic achievement is the hallmark of our education system, our school social environment holds significant sway in our development particularly where associated with play and socialization. Our basic social development begins here, often by establishment of rules of conduct and behavior in the classroom and expectations of society which are instructed, supervised and controlled by our teachers (primarily externally). It is in this environment in which we learn empathic behaviors associated with relationship skills, where great importance is put on aspects of play and socialization, but little on conflict management, negotiation and resolution. These skills are seldom developed as an essential social skill for adults and particularly so for adults within a relationship. Deficiencies initiated here that are not identified and corrected cascade into subsequent developmental stages and increase in severity.

In high school we transcend into adolescence and puberty. Erikson identified the stages associated with individual identity and intimacy as pivotal developmental issues for this stage of personal development. In this particular stage we become far more responsible for determining our own development, as the central questions of adolescence are "Who am I?" and "What role am I to play?" with each individual accountable for making that decision themselves. It will be here that we begin to pull away from the central authority figures of our parents, family, teachers, former peer groups and society at large. It is in this stage that we truly begin to self-conceptualize who we are based on our past experiences and perceived choices and paths before us, as we endeavor to determine our identity in combination with our emerging sexuality.

During this stage, individuals who are rejected socially or who are made to feel inadequate in relation to their peers will often develop a persistent sense of inferiority culminating with significant and frequently life-long self-esteem issues and poor self-conceptualization. Individuals who have developed healthy and virtuous self-concepts have remarkably little problems developing and engaging in healthy and virtuous relationships with others. Where this healthy self-concept fails to materialize, a sense of diminished self-esteem can lead individuals to fall particularly short of their potential particularly when developing social connections, as they will be naturally compelled to make fewer attempts to be social and as a consequence be less successful due to the lack of practice and a limited success rate. Furthermore, they will take benign rejection or social missteps as monumental failures, promoting additional social isolation. This isolation promotes a negative feedback loop in which healthy socialization and subsequent social skills are rarely developed, let alone realized. Isolation doesn't just occur with in-kind groups, but also when peer groups as a whole develop social cultures that reject civilizing values, behaviors and norms that promote stability, security and reduced tensions. As a result, whole groups are at a significant deficit in advancing healthy and virtuous relationship structures within their communities and suffer the cultural and community consequences resulting from these as a result.

It will be inadequacies at this stage where individuals will have profound and markedly poor socialization skill development that they will carry with them into adulthood. While it might not rise to the level to meet the diagnostic criteria for antisocial personality disorder, they very well could be border line.

Individuals here will exhibit poor judgment and an inability to learn from social experiences. They will lose insight into the complexities and involvement of other individual's feelings, positions or beliefs. They will fail to develop or follow any productive and viable life plan. They will have few connected friends or friendships and find it difficult to initiate such. Juvenile narcissism will run rampant. This narcissism will ferment social and civil resentment to include an unwillingness to develop and mature as an individual. Their sexual life and sexual identity will tend to be impersonal, trivial and poorly integrated.

Beauty, Power, Sex and Fame Don't Last

For those individuals higher on the Natural Selection axis but lower on Social Selection, without looking deeper at their personality, their relationship and social skills may appear to be in order and working. This is because of the compensatory effect of beauty, power, sex and fame, which generate biological signals that can often trump reason and virtue. We're naturally predisposed to respond positively to these traits. It's a fact of life. Beauty sells. Power sells. Sex sells. Fame sells. Because of this, you've been able to mask, hide and deflect a weakness of personality and character strength – up to this point.

Why should you change? When you already have beauty, power, sex or fame, plus the opportunities and time to leverage them, why engage in a personality overhaul that will take years, vast pools of energy and consistent effort to perform? You know the answer. We all really do and we're loath to bring it up or face it head on. How many examples of the extremely wealthy, the fabulously famous, the stunningly beautiful and the tyrannically powerful people's lives are nothing but a house of cards, are in shambles and end horrifically? How many of these people have we held admiration for but now pity in death? It is but a rare example of any individual to carry themselves throughout their lives and into their passing with grace, dignity and admiration. To do so will certainly require more than the base elements of Natural Selection but will undoubtably draw upon the deep resources available found within Social Selection. What's worse, is that you're not them. You don't have their wealth, fame, beauty or power. Granted the greater the heights, the greater the fall, but fall you will. Our lives are tragic in nature; we all die, our opportunities fleeting, our time in this life incredibly finite and wholly unguaranteed.

Developing a solid self-concept, relationship skills and filtering and selecting for a relationship partner whose values, and behaviors manifest these is a form of relationship insurance; or more aptly put, relationship ensurence.

They essentially sustain life of and for the relationship. Relationship skills by their nature seek to reduce the stress, remove doubt, suspend fear, to guard against loss, and to provide for a desired outcome. Beauty, power, sex, and fame are all ephemeral, if there is any fear in you that these will fade and effect your quality of life (and they will fade) you cannot permit yourself to wait until it's too late to change the course of life from what you're facing to what you could have had.

Deeply seated at the basic level, similar adverse life events, impaired development and childhood experiential factors are at play as well, from the fundamental level, but are not as overwhelming. Individuals in the category of being high on Natural Selection traits and low in Social Selection traits typically focus around a failure or misstep in a single or pair of factors in the social development phases, rather than an acute and encompassing deficiency in individual social maturation. As such, there is increasing probability of mitigating and resolving these deficiencies into normalized social development through awareness, dedicated work and practice.

Individuals who have been thwarted in the healthy resolution of earlier phases of child-to-adult development, such as learning healthy levels of trust, autonomy, self-identity etc., can expect to see these same problems reappear in the future in their adult lives. Where we stop progressing or have significant voids in our development, these are the skill sets we carry into our adult lives. Since no parent can teach us completely what we need. We often arrive at adulthood having never attained great portions of what is required to be ourselves in a healthy and productive manner. We're simply underdeveloped children in fully developed bodies, and act and behave according to our woman-child or man-child level of development and maturity.

> Nowhere is this more profound than when an individual is under pressure and stressed, such as at the center of conflict. Because children who are exposed to several adverse experiences and contexts tend to be overloaded with stress hormones, leaving them

in a constant limbic state of fight or flight. This then tends to be their primary behavioral response pattern associated with stress. When our needs are not met, when boundaries are violated, when expectations go unfulfilled, it is not uncommon for individuals to resort to their comfort zone of behavior and to utilize the skill sets associated with their level of personal social development: yelling, screaming, name calling, rage, overt displays at offense and anger, throwing things, slamming doors, pouting and general child-like high drama temper tantrums and storming out. Why? Because you know nothing else and it works. It worked in childhood. It's worked in the past. It works for now - at least it did, until all the adults in your life have simply left the room and you're left with nothing but your child-like developmental friends and associates. And you simply wash yourself of those that have given offense, rinse off any accountability you played in the relationship, reaffirm your sense of value of yourself and repeat the scenario over again, and again and again, hoping for change that doesn't seem to come. It happens because your developmental failures have grown into a personality disorder which you now own and it limits your abilities to function in relationships and other areas of life requiring similar socialization and socialization skills. To do otherwise, is to be stuck in the hurt zone catering to men of lesser character and ability or alone with the company of your cat, a bottle of wine and Facebook.

The Examined Life

Your attachment and focus on Natural Selection traits & attributes (beauty, power, sex and fame) are your attempts to primarily resolve internal conflicts (psychological developmental stage deficiencies, trauma and neglect) by way of external elements (beauty, power, sex and fame). The problem is external factors cannot resolve internal issues of insecurity, dependency or lack of love. Because of this you will always be a prisoner to that which you fail to confront.

People need a practical way to reframe their lives and their lifestyles in order to create healthy relationships, rather than live in such a way to maintain and support poor ones. Unfortunately, we cannot change or heal what we do not acknowledge. It is for this reason that finding and resolving hidden dependency needs (which are indicators of deficiencies in developmental stages) is essential. A simple beginning is to start a developmental journal/record of your past and personal history. Analyze your emotional needs and what drives them. What issues do you think will be fulfilled by any new relationship? Most likely they will be issues of personal development and self-identity that you have not fulfilled or fully actualized. Learning to identify and addressing those will have profound ramifications for your personal growth and quality of life, as it gets projected into the future, by the decisions and choices you make for yourself.

Although one can do the introspection, analysis, reading and research to help identify and resolve these personal developmental tasks, often it is vastly more efficient and effective to hire a professional trained specifically in the areas of social psychological development. Their ability and training to be objective in seeing and helping to piece together the parts and pieces of your life, particularly those elements that are missing, can often relieve you of years of emotional burdens. While it's expensive, it is not as expensive as the untracked costs of NOT doing so (see the carnage of deep interpersonal relationships that have failed). These professionals are trained, familiar and practiced at providing assistance, specifically in the developmental tasks you need the most. They are prepared to see what you might prefer to avoid and assist you at arriving at deeper and more meaningful insights about your relationships, yourself and your past for you to move ahead productively, in a healthy and secure manner.

Another incredible step is changing the perspective in which you view yourself and your past by the manner in which you treat yourself today and in this very moment. By changing how you treat yourself, your past and your development you alter the most important element in the entire equation of developing and fostering healthy and productive relationships... YOU! You must be the agent of change for yourself. No one else can fix you. You're an adult now, which means taking care of your own needs and choosing a responsible path of action and being accountable to those choices. Your journey starts with you. Begin there. The most important step of any journey is the first one.

"The unexamined life is not worth living"
-Socrates (the Original)

Exploring our psychological makeup is often utilized for the spiritual development within ourselves, as it leads to an awakening of the consciousness about us, our natures and our possibilities. One cannot understand what is left unexamined. Most people only have a superficial observation of their own lives. They understand only the tip of the iceberg, but remain ignorant to the vast extent of the psychological subliminal forces that are actually directing and influencing control of their conscious self.   It is these explorations, I feel, that lead to true self confidence and self-awareness.

The only common denominator in all of your relationships is you. Taking the time to understand what drives your behavior, needs, wants and desires for the relationship, and within them, can, and frequently does, result in finding dependency needs that are lurking within your psyche and sense of personal identity and personal narrative. These traits, more than likely, have been the underlying fault in any of the relationships you have been in, including the last one. By examining your past relationships, you are in effect utilizing them as a psychological mirror to yourself. To be able to look beyond the immediacy of your self-projected identity and more deeply into the identity of the person who is really driving the decisions you make for yourself and your life. This is an immense tool for discovering and resolving these often deeply seated issues.

Relationships usually die slow deaths: a series of broached boundaries, violated expectations, broken promises and poor behavior that lead up to a building resentment within the parties. Normally there is vastly more to it than the the idea that somebody was "unhappy" or a specific deal killing issue or betrayal came about. By performing the relationship autopsy you are looking for the underlying choices, behaviors and actions that lead to the demise of that relationship. Once identified, the next task, in each case, is to determine what was driving those choices, behaviors and actions, how they came to be and how are they manifesting themselves now. These dependency needs will point directly toward deficiencies within your personal developmental stages. You will need to address these, which will often reopen old and deeply felt trauma that is truly yet unresolved. By addressing the underlying drivers (developmental stages), you will resolve the plethora of symptoms that they ultimately manifest.   Seek to address the causes, not the symptoms of the choices, behaviors and actions that lead to self-defeating patterns of behavior within yourself and your relationships.

The value of taking stock of yourself, your life, those to whom your care was obligated, your friends, your peer groups and your personal relationships is that it reveals to you a lot about who you are and what developmental tasks (what you're trying to learn, develop and grow from) you have left. If you pause to evaluate these relationships you can see what your next developmental tasks will likely be and can then choose a partner who is more appropriate , both in terms of your emotional preferences in life and values and your growing edge of personal development of being. These types of choices almost without a fault lead to healthier and more fulfilling relationships than those selected and based only upon attraction and arousal.

The MAP- A Personal Guide to the Sexual Marketplace

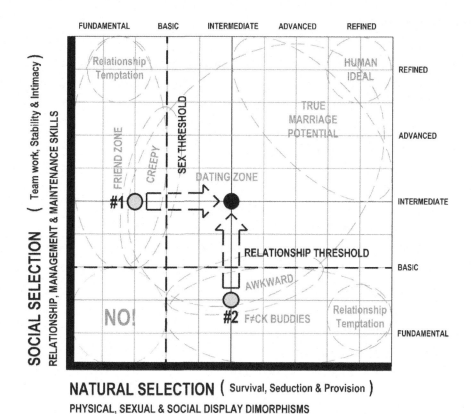

FUNDAMENTAL   BASIC   INTERMEDIATE   ADVANCED   REFINED

NATURAL SELECTION (Survival, Seduction & Provision)
PHYSICAL, SEXUAL & SOCIAL DISPLAY DIMORPHISMS

Micro Utilization

In previous sections on the Map Utilization we've identified how to approximate your specific position within the sexual marketplace based on the two of the greatest drivers of the sexual marketplace (Natural Selection and Social Selection), identified what your long-term goals and objectives are (where you really want to be within the sexual marketplace) and outlined the appropriate course of actions to take to achieve these goals and why. These ideas were presented in large scale (Macro) environment both in overall behavioral and temporal (time) context. What we now will focus on is that the very same factors that aided us in the Macro environment will be the exact same factors that will be utilized in a Micro environment - the one-on-one individual actions within a singular interpersonal interaction.

This would be a great time to review the initial section on utilization of our map. The graphic above is the exact same one we discussed earlier and it will be relevant whether we are discussing how we are observed over a long period of time or whether it is over a single interaction with a given individual or group in the moment.

To quickly summarize that section:
- Identify where you are at, and in particular, if you are sliding into another zone within a specific interaction or conversation!
- Understand where you want to go - which direction and axis.
- Respect the vector. Your responses have to be on the same plane as the axis of movement toward your goal.
- Remove the negatives first - the obvious detrimental behaviors you're currently exhibiting.
- Apply basic response elements first.
- Increase the skill complexity proportionally.

The Basics of Micro Utilization (WHY)

You're in the zone you're in because of the things you are doing, presenting and communicating that tell the market that's where you belong, not just long term and over time, but specifically RIGHT NOW! The elements that position you long term in any zone, are the same elements that are providing in the moment evidence for your categorization on a case by case basis. These micro expressions of behavior, actions and displays cumulatively add up to your macro expression (overall brand). Learning to manage these during a moment to moment interaction is the starting point for any modifications moving forward. After all, relationships are made from one person to another and are built up over time. They are a result of patterns of behavior (that become expected) and nodes of specific instances that serve as defining moments. These define our perceptions of individuals as well as our expected interactions and our relationships with them.

Understanding this, knowing where you are currently positioned and where you'd like to be, you have an immediate action plan on what you can do RIGHT NOW to modify those perceptions.

Your brand is negotiated within the sexual marketplace. Your behaviors and manner in which you present yourself within this market establishe your brand, both long term and with each individual you connect with. How are you interacting with each market contact that reflects that brand and their interpretation and impressions of it and you? In business terms, what is your customer service like and how are they responding? Great company brands don't have poor customer service for long, in fact, great company brands are KNOWN for their great customer service and support.

We should also acknowledge two things. The first is that your particular zone is your comfort zone, in other words, the area you are most at ease and where you feel the safest. Individuals in the Friend Zone are most comfortable utilizing Social Selection traits and attributes and those individuals in the Fuck Buddy Zone are most comfortable with the Natural Selection traits and attributes. These will naturally the skill set you will utilize when pressured or stressed. The second thing to remember is that overcoming this inclination will not only be difficult to resist, but will feel uncomfortable. This is why practice is so important, because we default to our training and natural patterns of behavior, particularly when we are not paying attention to them, or when we are seeking security when we are facing stiff market realities opposing us.

- When it occurs, recognize the situation for what it is and self arrest.
- Break your habit. Know what you need to do rather than what you would like to do.
- Get out from your comfort zone. Implement new skills that will change the situation.
- Validate yourself for these changes and get back to it again. Wash, rinse and repeat.

We should also point out that individuals in the Friend Zone or the Fuck Buddy Zone are both at a disadvantage, having fallen well behind their peers and there are three particular instances we need to understand and address before we get into particulars of either zone; those of back-sliding, getting out of debt and bad credit.

Backsliding- this is the instance where we are relapsing into our former habits or we discern that individuals are starting to perceive us to be placed in a particular zone, and not one of our preference. The immediate response should be to correct that by reinvesting into those traits and attributes appropriately in response to our individual zone. The problem is a single instance of doing so isn't going to overcome setting perceptions. We are going to have to compensate in kind appropriately in order to resist and reframe. This doesn't mean overcompensate in a single grand expression, but to make amends or counter balance those perceptions by displaying the appropriate ones accordingly, in scale and at the appropriate level. If you're in the Friend Zone and catch yourself in poor posture, its better to correct the posture than to try to overcompensate and have 'grand posture' that comes off as posing or cartoonish. Likewise, if you're in the Fuck Buddy Zone and you find yourself indicating your ill-suited nature towards relationships, correct your course by engaging in pro-relationship telegraphing that is not sexual. Taking an interest in feeding someone's soul through cooking isn't the same as preparing sexual hors d'oeuvres.

Social researchers have noted that to offset a single negative experience, several (usually four) positive experiences need to occur. Please keep in mind that this would theoretically bring us back to a neutral state of mind, not quite the positive result that we're aiming for. In other words, we are going to have to consistently make these positive adjustments to offset a resulting or expected negative view point of us, consistently and over a period of time.

Getting out of debt- individuals in either zone are deeply in social debt, either established by not being sexually desirable or by being bereft of relationship potential. In either case, both groups are severely in the hole.

Much like being financially in a the hole, we must focus on what got us there in the first place. Most people who are in debt focus relentlessly on the accounting, the numbers. The problem is, the numbers didn't cause the debt. People's behaviors did. Likewise, we will need to focus on what got us into this situation, our behaviors, and not the accounting system itself. Much how getting into monetary debt isn't typically just a single instance of overspending, but a sustained behavioral pattern of living beyond our means, so too is getting into social debt. If we expect to get out of debt we need to stop over spending (ineffectual relationship behavior), start saving to pay down that debt (incremental positive behavior) and increase our income (increasing our abilities and skill sets).

Bad Credit- much like your financial credit history, we have established social history. Those individuals who are so far in debt and have exhibited such poor financial judgment pose little concern or risk; there is none, because people don't take risks with known negatives. Those people don't get access to others resources. Those deep in the Friend Zone don't get sexual access and those deep in the Fuck Buddy Zone don't get relationship access. The risk occurs with those individuals who are sub-prime, not completely lost causes, either sexually or relationship wise. As we previously noted in the section on the Map Zones, they are facing the obstacles associated with being creepy or awkward. The risk associated with these obstacles are the incongruent behaviors associated with not being in a fully stabilized and accepted role, which builds tension, risk and internal conflict in decision making until resolved. This internal conflict will then warrant and garner additional scrutiny and attention for the lender. You are going to be even more under review rather than less. Much like applying for a loan, those with a poor financial track record will have to fill out more paper work, and more than likely receive subprime lending rates (increased scrutiny) in return. Much like fixing your credit score, you will need to express and display the following; agency and congruent, consistent behavior improvement.

Friend Zoned

The MAP- A Personal Guide to the Sexual Marketplace

Individuals in the Friend Zone exhibit too many of the Social Selection traits and too few of the Natural Selection traits. This is true for their overall reputation, as well as individual interactions between individuals. Generally your interactions lack the following Natural Selection traits and attributes:

Physical dimorphisms- you don't look or sub-communicate the part of a sexually confident, grown individual.

Social dimorphisms - you lack standing and value to the social group in which you're involved. You are largely passive and unresponsive socially. You simply lack presence, confidence and standing as a result.

Sexual dimorphisms - You don't exhibit nor spark sexual attention, interest or arousal. You're weak in identifying and presenting Indicators of Interest (IOIs): those behavior traits of flirtation, teasing and banter that signal sexual interest and receptivity.

To change this situation within a personal interaction you will need to respond in kind and specifically in those areas of Natural selection in which you are the weakest, as they will proffer the greatest response potential.

Physical dimorphisms- If you don't look or sub-communicate the part of a sexually confident grown individual, change that! Sit up, stand up, learn to take up emotional and physical space. Physically communicate that you're not ashamed, embarrassed or intimidated. Look people in the eye that you are talking to. Learn to emotionally take up space. Have and express your opinion, particularly where it differs from others. Begin to express in words and physical form that you matter. Start realizing that you are a heroic being and your body posture should reflect that. Stop slouching, turning away, looking down, and generally acting sheepish. Provide a presence, showcase confidence and personal eminence instead. Learn to develop socially acceptable forms social touch, to develop personal connection and rapport, as well as, to accentuate a social moment or point, appropriately.

Social dimorphisms – If you lack standing and value to the social group in which you're involved change that too! Look to provide social value, instead of taking it or being afraid to risk rejection in the process. Individuals who are Natural Selection trait orientated are not passive or unresponsive socially, but you are. Change that. Have an opinion. Voice it. Double-down on it when challenged and then exaggerate that position to comic level for obvious humor and self-amusement. Your natural predisposition is to reduce tension, anxiety and to increase social stability, but that's not particularly fun, exciting or novel in a social setting. Learning to appropriately increase social tension, anxiety and to decrease social stability in fun, exciting and novel ways provides value. It's called being playful, having fun or teasing. There is tremendous advantage to non-sexual teasing and banter socially. Learn to be socially engaging in the patterns of play, showcase a lack of impulse control and predictability in your interactions. Learn to socially stop a failing negative social thread such as whining, complaining or bitching. Learn to say "No!" playfully. Let him or her shower their life's complaints on their friends and family. Learn to say "No Ma'am!" or "No, Sir!", "Stop it!", "Behave yourself!", "Shhh!", "this is the inner circle of fun - no complaining", to reframe your interaction into something playful instead of something serious. Remember that the strongest frame will win. This doesn't mean to continually escalate, but when their price point to continue exceeds an appropriate threshold, stop playing altogether. Disengage. This could be a playful back turn, or a serious one. Don't chase, don't pursue, don't engage. Introduce them to someone else. Playfully let them know who to complain and bitch to; "Where are your parents??? Are they here? Do I need to get them?" You can replace parents for friends or allude to an imaginary boyfriend or girlfriend. You know they don't have one, not acting like this. You could also throw that in there too. "THIS is why you don't have a partner!" Just be careful not to burn a bridge and if you do, DON'T supplicate. Then you're proving it was only an act and you'll embolden them later.

If having fun is fun, how do you increase the fun factor? Intentionally misbehave. There's fun and then there's misbehaving fun, doing something that you shouldn't do to bring on added delight. Remember that being serious in a social context isn't being social, it's you being serious, which is boring. Another particularly poor social trait that you're exhibiting is that of outcome dependence; the conscious desire for a specific outcome and fear associated with rejection or failure in its absence. This outcome dependence is sub-communicating an incredible neediness and emotional dependency upon others which is value taking, rather than value providing and people will ultimately reject you for it. Stop it. Be willing to open up, express yourself, be self-amused and face social disapproval openly as a form of risk taking and personal development. What you'll find is excellent raw data to analyze and reframe for a better approach, delivery and content.

Sexual dimorphisms – if you don't exhibit nor spark sexual attention, interest or arousal, you're not likely to elicit it from someone else either. Furthermore, if you're weak in identifying and presenting Indicators of Interest, you are going to find it incredibly difficult and come across as creepy when you express sexual or romantic interest. The alternative and vastly more successful approach is to learn what elements spark sexual attention, interest and arousal in your specific market niche and how to go about eliciting that from your target audience. Within this context you're going to have to learn what the behavioral indicators of interest are, realize that they are being directed at you in response to your social interaction with them and then how to initiate or reciprocate those same signals appropriately to the individual you have interest in. The key here is not some grand gesture. That's too desperate, needy and risky in all the wrong ways. What you're trying to do is to open the door to the naturally occurring and appropriately human sexual interests in other individuals. This should not be a deluge of signals, advances or off-handed remarks, but a pinging - a signal that questions if there is a connection or interest. Our focus should be seeing if it is received, how it is received and if it is reciprocated in turn. This is very much like the concept of sharing; is it mutual and if so is it matched equally. Much like sharing, there is the real danger and social faux pas of "over sharing" that is inappropriate. Unfortunately, one of the most difficult things individuals in the Friend Zone will ever have to do is to stop rejecting themselves and dismissing their sexuality and self interest in light of their potential partner's lack of it. Ultimately if you cannot represent your sexual interest you're broadcasting rather loudly that you're highly not likely to take care of theirs or other potential matches' interest as well. To complicate things when dealing with the Natural Selection axis, attraction, arousal and interest cannot be negotiated. You either have it or you don't. You're either fit to survive, provide and mate or you're not.

Before you run off and start applying greater Natural Selection traits and attributes throughout your interpersonal conversations and interactions let's make sure there's a degree of restraint and appropriate control with how you do so and the degree in which this is measured out. Your first and primary interest should be removing the negative behaviors and your non-verbal body language. The second is to increase the degree of Natural Selection traits appropriately. Remember that if you're in the Friend Zone, which is well below average. Jumping right into an advance social trait will be detrimental and incongruent behavior. We should initially be looking at advancing our behavior from below normal (our comfort zone) to normal expression of Natural Selection traits. Just doing this is going to be uncomfortable and challenging enough, but we are also going to need to do it consistently and over time. Our intention isn't just THIS particular social engagement, but ALL of our social engagements. We are trying to re-establish your personal baseline of comfort and will take time and effort to do so. Once you're in your new comfort zone and you're used to physical expression, socially playfulness and general sexual conveyance, then we can look to increase those proportionally.

Fuck Buddied

The MAP- A Personal Guide to the Sexual Marketplace

Individuals in the Fuck Buddy Zone are signaling and exhibiting for too much of the Natural Selection traits and cultural values of beauty, power, sex and fame and far too few of the Social Selection traits of team work, stability and (non-sexual) intimacy.

In doing so they are failing to appropriately communicate the values and virtues associated with being a potential partner, the ability to manage relationships or maintain them. This is true for their overall brand and as well as their individual conversations and interactions with others. Generally, their interpersonal interactions lack the following Social Selection traits and attributes that would indicate that they would not make honest and appropriate friends let alone be relationship potential:

Team Work- The social capability and skills associated with team building, of being an appropriate partnership choice, an inability to self-regulate and display long-term thinking over short-term, the empathic socialized behaviors of caring, consideration and the aptitude for reducing tension, anxiety and conflict within any relationship structure.

Relationship Stability- the inability to adequately manage interactions of unspoken relationship expectations of trust, respect and personal boundaries essential for relationship consistency and permanence and the failure to demonstrate self-restraint of emotional impulse control and rational behavior, instead resorting to defensive and aggressive emotional behaviors associated with 'fight or flight' responses and limbic associated behavior.

Intimacy- the incapability to showcase talent for the relationship maintenance of meeting another individual's physical, emotional and psychological needs and appropriately sustaining those throughout the course of a relationship.

People are constantly signaling and telling others who they are, what they are about and what we can expect from them on almost a continued basis and, based on this, we can and do categorize them rather rapidly. Individuals in the Fuck Buddy Zone are consistently either sub-communicating or overtly communicating that they are completely into themselves, are incredibly short-sighted, lack an ability to limit, reduce or diffuse tension, are unable to appropriately manage trust, respect or personal boundaries, let alone attempt to do with others and have very limited connection and bonding attributes aside from tantalization, escapism and sex. Is it any wonder that out of these exhibited traits tantalization, escapism and sex is the consistent value with which you attract all of your relationships? The truth is you're not showcasing much else. The problem is that the Social Selection traits and attributes need to be taught, whereas the Natural Selection traits and attributes are biologically driven and rewarded.

We are all familiar with the Natural Selection traits and attributes presented on display when screening for attraction, provision and seduction, because they are first and foremost biological and specifically at a limbic level (our oldest and evolutionary most developed brain structure), which means those responses will be acute and immediate (our survival depends upon this). What won't be so acute and far more negotiable, will be the Social Selection indicators, because they reside in our mammalian portion of our brain and our cerebral cortex; that portion of our brain that distinctly has evolved to develop rational thought and decision-making processes that differentiates us from the rest of the animal kingdom. It is this brain structure that has evolved to give us the ability to comprehend, understand, rationalize and navigate the increasing complex social structures developed by man to survive and provide for himself and his offspring. These are man-made social structures, not biological ones and as such they need to be taught, learned and developed. So too, do we need to incorporate our decision-making responses in favor of them beyond our biological inclinations associated with Natural selection. This is the area in which individuals in the Fuck Buddy Zone are failing horribly. They simply are not leveraging the tremendous value of Social Selection traits and attributes into their lives appropriately. Individuals actively screening and filtering for healthy, virtue-based relationships will screen for these by observing behavior, what you say, do and how you present yourself and also by asking and juxtaposing stated value with behavior. Nothing showcases personal values like personal behavior (listen to what people say but watch what they do). Individuals in the Fuck Buddy Zone are simply showcasing themselves, as not being relationship material overall and specifically within individual interpersonal interactions. To change that situation, we need to specifically focus on those areas you are least aware, and least capable of and redress those.

Team Work- within your interpersonal interactions you are displaying a lack of social capability and skills associated with appropriate socialization and team building ability. Notably, your behaviors and display presentation are associated with a high degree of narcistic self-interest (beauty, power, sex & fame), entitlement, sophomoric sarcasm and juvenile social skills associated with empathy and behaviors of reducing tensions, anxieties and conflicts socially, namely caring, consideration and respect.

Relationship Stability- your interpersonal skills associated with relationship stabilization or relationship management abilities are poor at best. On a regular basis you will be showcasing a suspension of personal accountability and likely will be proud and fond of those behaviors, as you'll be perceiving those as independence and free spiritedness. But the bottom line is you can't manage yourself. You can't manage a relationship with others and chafe when others attempt to manage you. You will also demonstrate an inability to adequately manage interactions of unspoken relationship expectations of trust, respect and personal boundaries essential for committed monogamous relationships and their consistency and permanence. In short, you're still shopping, and you convey that in words and deeds. You will also express a previous history of relationship failure associated with infidelity and there will be no overt display at resolution, self-introspection, self-knowledge and development that should have come from the expense of that relationship. Instead you will display staggering lack of agency and accountability associated with that failure moving forward. Lastly you will also convey a lack self-restraint of emotional impulse control and rational behavior, instead resorting to defensive and aggressive emotional behaviors associated with "fight or flight" responses. This will ultimately extend to unwitting acknowledgement of your inability to control or manage your biological impulse for hypergamy and hypogamy.

Intimacy- your interpersonal skills associated with relationship maintenance is focused primarily on short-term biological and hormonal mechanism of bonding resulting from a genetic predisposition to mate and little on the social elements that sustain relationships, preserve the quality and balance the dialectic tensions (values that appear to be opposing in nature) within a relationship. Very little of your time, consideration or effort will be placed on preventive relationship maintenance care. If any exists, it will be centered on your managing your relationship value supply (what you want out of the relationship) and little to none of the tending to mutual relationship value and direction that supports the relationship. Equally, you will be unlikely to take serious efforts to sustain your relationship in the form of nurturing, supporting and feeding it. You will not make concerted and consistent efforts associated with relationship stabilization, quality (theirs not yours), preserving relationship status standards (interest, empathy, affection, etc,) and balancing the naturally occurring tensions associated between opposite values; connectedness vs autonomy, predictability vs novelty etc.

In being aware that in our daily interactions we are sub communicating and often overtly communicating that we are and would make poor relationship choices by not being caring, considerate and empathic, failing to self-regulate long-term values over short-term values, and failing to develop personal rapport and connection with others. In doing so we remove ourselves from the potentiality of the relationships we are naturally inclined to have and desire. A key starting point is our very next involvement with someone else. Stop placing your immediate needs first and think about what the relationship between the two of you really needs to develop. The first and most beneficial thing isn't something that we will add, but something that we will remove; the negative elements that are undermining our relationships. We need to stop being such and bitch and stop being a dick. The next step will be looking squarely at those areas of Social Selection that you are the weakest and applying the elements in the following chapter that corresponds with those. The key here is to not focus on the higher skill levels or abilities but moving your understanding and application (mastery) from below average to average. If you can apply yourself at doing both (self-arresting poor behavior, then developing simple skills you're not used to applying), they in turn will dramatically change the way you are perceived and valued not only as a friend, but also as a potential partner.

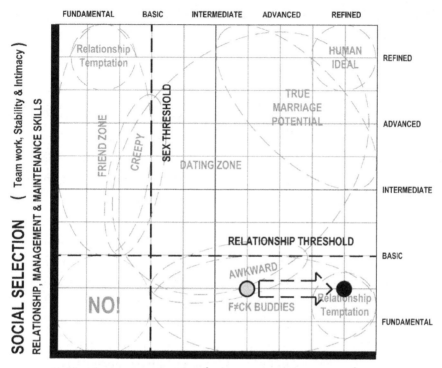

NATURAL SELECTION (Survival, Seduction & Provision)
PHYSICAL, SEXUAL & SOCIAL DISPLAY DIMORPHISMS

Common Failures; Hot or Not!

Hot or Not! Or why exhibiting traits and attributes within the Natural Selection category; being hotter, wealthier, powerful and famous, doesn't make for a good long-term relationship strategy and nor is it in your best life-long interests.

Before we begin let's recap what the Natural Selection Traits are. They are those traits and attributes associated with:

Survival- the various human markers associated with physical dimorphisms of an individual such as physical stature, general health and overall fitness.

Seduction- the displays of deliberate sexual enticement, sexual provocation and sexual execution.

Provision- the various societal markers associated with standing or social rank, displays of wealth, power and fame.

So, what is wrong with an over or outright emphasis of Natural Selection when it comes to a guiding principal to self-improvement and your offerings in the sexual marketplace? Well, for starters, Natural Selection is a mating strategy, not a relationship strategy. If you are interested in your long-term interests, having a romantic partner who will be a benefit in your life in reducing stress, tensions, anxieties, provide stability, comfort, nurturing support and has the ability to maintain and sustain that relationship over the course of your life, you need to select for that and those traits, which are Social Selection traits, not Natural Selection traits. Increasing your sexual and mating desirability are the hallmarks of Natural Selection. When you emphasize sexuality, you shouldn't be surprised when those looking for sexual traits are attracted to what you're promoting. For people below average, when it comes to relationship skills, management ability and maintenance practices, (which is half of us) you just can't get to having committed long-term relationships by only emphasizing Natural Selection Traits of whether you're 'Hot or Not' (see graph). The same is true for those people (typically men) who focus on wealth and power. Likewise, for both men and women who choose to pursue fame.

So why all the misplaced emphasis by so many people? Well, simply because we're genetically engineered for it. Sex, sexual attraction, wealth, power, fame and sexualized behavior attract and command a disproportionate amount of biological interest, attention and response... initially. It's supposed to! Nature intended to develop our "natural" biological responses as a short-term reproduction and species survival mechanism. It's literally encoded into our genetics. In other words, it's natural. Left to our own brutish instincts this is the manner in which nature would have us survive and mate and so many of us do, or at least try. That is, until either we fail or are so traumatized by our errors that we learn from those experiences.

Let's look at a few of the reasons why being focused solely on natural selection traits is selling short on your potential and birthright.

The Sexual Marketplace as a Commodity Exchange

The primary challenge facing those who put their focus on Natural Selection attributes of being hotter/fitter, wealthier, more powerful and famous is that the values they entice and elicit to make a relationship happen are all based on you being a high value commodity (product) in a saturated marketplace. Within the Natural Selection category elements, people unsurprisingly focus on their attractiveness and sexuality, as the improvements applied here are obvious and results immediate. It's something we understand, have command of and have been constantly inundated with, unlike wealth, power and fame, which are more foreign to us and seemingly out of our control. Because sex and sexuality are the most prolific of the Natural Selection categories, these expressed values become the default currency in which people exchange to entice, captivate, establish and keep a relationship, which leads to a number of horrifying ramifications where you compete based on your ability to attract by increase offerings, willingness to undercut the competition, maintain an aging product (you) that decreases in value with time and thrive in a cultural by-product of this environment, by exhibiting the dark-triad traits of narcissism, sociopathy and Machiavellianism.

Increased Offerings and Price Centric Race to the Bottom

In any market, goods and services compete by distinguishing themselves first by capturing the consumer's attention. In the sexual marketplace this is explicitly linked to hypergamy and hypogamy. Men and women are going to have to brand, exhibit and market themselves based on the desires and values of their customer base and within the Natural Selection category where sex and sexuality is the primary currency. As such, you are going to have to sexually brand (create a sexual identity), market (successfully telegraph and convey your value/promise to your target audience) and successfully execute a sale to your customer base. For half of us, our abilities within each of these realms are average or lacking and our competition are our betters.

Everyone wants to be the high-cost, high-quality option within the sexual marketplace, but for that to happen we actually have to **BE** a high-value, high quality option within the sexual marketplace. This is going to take substantial work, effort and dedication to achieve (which I know you're already aware of) and runs the risk of being undercut perpetually, or we can go to market with the product we have and enhance our services (increase value) and undercut our competition, by being the low-cost, high value option of being a slut or player, which is so endemic in today's sexual marketplace.

Ladies, you know all too well how difficult, challenging and consuming it is to maintain, let alone enhance your sexual desirability amongst men, only to have your efforts undercut by your sluttier, whorish brethren, who not only are all too willing to put out sexually, but increase the value of it through refined ability and value added sexual services. This is one of the primary reasons why a blowjob is the new kiss goodnight in today's sexual marketplace, and sex on the first date is commonplace, if not standard practice. Where anal sex and threesomes were once taboo, they are now deal sealers. But that isn't quite enough is it? With the prolific developments in technology driving the sheer availability of pornography, which has the effect of raising the bar of sexual expectations, to the plethora of social media vastly increasing available options that you have to compete against and the content you need to provide in the form of sexual selfies.

Ladies, you primarily have three options: quit and forfeit your birthright of having the relationship you desire, stop playing the Natural Selection game and develop and select for Social Selection traits, or really step up your Natural Selection game and become that hotter, fitter and vastly more sexually aggressive and adventurous self that the bad-boys you favor choose. To do otherwise, is to be stuck in the hurt zone catering to men of lesser character and ability or alone with the company of your cat, a bottle of wine and Facebook.

Guys, in general we have it a whole lot easier here. With the quality, availability and endless supply of younger, hotter, fitter women who are more and more willing to be overly sexualized and sexual, it is truly a remarkable period to be an even a half-assed player. Call it a "player's renaissance". Our biggest concern is to keep the sexual hopper filled and operating (all too easy with social digital media), not getting attached (be warned - nature and biology are stacked against you here) and controlling our insecurities, self-esteem and anger levels below the violence level (for those with low Social Selection traits and abilities this will be a nearly impossible task) when we allow our player stature to slip. All this comes with two forewarnings: don't shake a whore-tree and expect a wife to fall out and realize that the highs of your life are vapid, the lows all the more devastating when we are cast away in self-induced isolation. We reap what we sow.

The ravages associated with time
If sex and sexuality (primary currency within natural selection) is such an awesome driving biological factor, where's the problem, particularly when we all naturally want, desire and are rewarded for pursuing and indulging those things? The problem is that all of the elements that make up Natural Selection are all perishable; they

simply don't last and constitute the cycle of life. We can rail against time, but time always eclipses us. We simply don't live forever and thus we don't have forever.

- We physically deteriorate...
- Our fitness levels worsen...
- Our health levels diminish...
- Our social standings do not last...
- Our sources of power are fleeting...
- Our sources of wealth are limited...
- Our sources of fame evaporate...

and we "naturally" lose tremendous sexual value because of all of it. During the course of the average life span, this period in which we are most valued for our natural selection traits and attributes is terribly limited and too frequently squandered out of ignorance. We simply falsely believe that the same choices and opportunities that we have in our youth will be in full effect or better later in our lives.

The Dark Triade of Narcissism, Sociopathy and Machiavellianism

A cultural by-product of a society, culture and individuals that focus on and rewards those traits associated with Natural Selection is that it increases utilization and acceptance of behavioral traits known as the dark-triad, which are profoundly successful when untethered from civilizing behaviors associated with Social Selection. The dark-triad comprise the mindset and behavioral actions of individuals associated with a high level of narcistic exhibition, the anti-social, moral irresponsibility and lack of social conscience associated with sociopathy and the employment of cunning and duplicity in behavior associated with Machiavellianism.

Narcissism - pursuit of gratification from vanity or egotistic admiration of one's own attributes and abilities; physical beauty and fitness, wealth, power and fame.

Sociopathy and Psychopathy - personality disorder traits that are characterized by enduring antisocial and cultural behaviors, diminished empathy and a lack of conscience and remorse. It also includes a high level of impulsivity, selfishness, callousness and lack of self-control.

Machiavellianism - employment of cunning and duplicity in social governance or general behavioral conduct. Manipulation and exploitation of others and a cynical disregard for morality and focus on self-interest and deception are all hallmarks of relationship management that frame their relationship structures.

What is becoming rather startling with society is that these behavioral traits are pronounced within both sexes, where it was presumed that only males primarily exhibited these traits. These traits simply hold true for both sexes when either places a premium on Natural Selection. Furthermore, we should also be prepared to reap what we sow. When we place a premium on Natural Selection traits for relationship partner choice, we can anticipate that our partners will represent and exhibit those behavioral traits that best meet those needs; the dark-triad. Just as we exhibit them, but so too will our mate choice. Morally we also cannot honestly expect others to treat us differently than how we treat and regard them. As such, are you really prepared and willing to enter into a 'committed' relationship with someone who is vain, exhibits a number of anti-social disorders such as a lack of empathy, caring or consideration and employs relationship management principles that involve cunning and duplicity? Or to reverse engineer your past relationship strategy, does this sound like your old or current relationship?

What's more is when you and your partner are low in the Social Selection traits and attributes you are unlikely or incapable of resolving conflicts peacefully, appropriately and to the betterment of both parties. When you lack these abilities, aggression and violence is the management method of choice because of its ease, effectiveness and our natural biological

The MAP- A Personal Guide to the Sexual Marketplace

predisposition to it. If you can't manage a relationship appropriately, you will manage it inappropriately and the last skill that is reached for when no others are available, trusted or can be relied on, is violence. This can be physical. It can be emotional. And it can be psychological. It can be material. It can and often does include not only the parties involved, but others as well, friends, family members and the worst, their own children weaponized to hurt their now rival partner. Just imagine a vicious divorce. All the elements too often are at play: battery, emotional and psychological harm and distress intentionally inflected via emotional withholding, lack of intimacy and ultimately adultery, the strip and seizure of material possessions, the manipulation of others to enlist in your service and side from friends and family, to the coercive control of the relationship in the form of the police and the willful destruction of the family bond (your ultimate future) by ways and means of emotionally poisoning of your own children against the other parent.

But remember; nature doesn't care. Caring is a human construct. A civilizing one. One in which you didn't value in yourself or the partner you chose and now you expect consideration where you placed so little previously. Tell me, how's that working for you? I hope you took an image to remind yourself of how "hot" your partner was and that it is enough to console you when the inevitable happens.

Frictional Costs

To be fair, hardly anyone is truly devoid of social skills or are truly a sociopath or a psychopath (but the numbers are alarming), and thus there is always hope that an individual will learn, grow and develop those skills to meet or exceed life's requirements to handle the context and situations they're presented, but a simple reality remains; Life is harder when you're stupid or stupid about it. Life is vastly more difficult when we complicate and burden ourselves with a lack of preparation, planning and practiced ability, for us, our partner and our relationships. By not having appropriately developed relationships skills, management abilities and maintenance capabilities we limit our range of options to enduring and persevering (complacency), repair (attempts to mend crises and failures) and disposal and replacement. .This is really rough stock and trade to be dealing with. How much better would our lives be if we actually had command of the myriad of relationships skills, management abilities and maintenance patterns that provide for stable, secure and deeply intimate relationships? How much better would our lives be if our partners valued the same and had those abilities as well? There's a cost to be paid when we do not develop our Social Selection abilities and while we recognize them when we experience the difficulties of our lives when these are in short supply, we rarely proactively prepare ourselves or our relationships beforehand.

Evolutionary Development

From a biological perspective when we focus predominantly on Natural Selection traits for partner selection, interestingly enough, we don't achieve our human potential. Our species has specifically evolved a larger and more developed brain structure than our primate cousins, particularly the neo frontal cortex or the rational, complex information, language conferring, abstract thinking, planning and perception portion of our brains. It is what truly makes us unique as a species and we have been incredibly successful because of it. Because of these elements, we have been able to create the most important construct for our continued existence; complex, interdependent social structures. No other creature has been able to leverage their social structures in the manner nor to the degree that we have. We simply have yet to be out competed. Not only that, but we keep getting better at forming greater and more encompassing social structures. Our social structures have evolved as well from small multi-generational family units to multi-family clans and tribes. Tribes evolved into larger communities and greater societies and societies into nations and civilizations that we recognize today. In short, there were tremendous advantages to be gained and then further exploited for our survival beyond the selection choices for Natural Selection both individually and collectively. But therein lies the rub. We have to CHOOSE for those selection choices.

We have to learn, utilize and train that rational portion of our brain structure that chooses rationally over emotional convenience and biological impulse. These skills, abilities and traits need to be taught, learned and practiced, but the benefits for doing so are the resulting difference between us and our primate cousins evolutionary, and in doing so it will affect nearly every other facet of your life, not just in romance. It has the power to greatly affect your life. The life of your children and thus the power to strengthen your genetic family tree.

Lost Opportunities
Not only do the elements of Natural Selection not last, they actually don't make us happy. How's that for a bum deal? All the elements of Natural Selection don't last and they don't make us happy long-term. Sure, life is vastly better with these things, but they don't soothe our natural need to connect with others, to share and to embrace others and to be embraced by them. As a species we are not solitary animals. We thrive in social groups. We need them. It is part of what makes us human. We're deficient when we lack these connections, social relationships and intimacy. The classics tell us, the literature of mankind screams it through the ages, all of the Natural Selection traits and attributes mean nothing when we are isolated, alone and lonely. By placing over weighted emphasis on Natural Selection traits and attributes we rob ourselves of the opportunities to find and create fulfilling, life affirming and biologically satisfying relationships that we're so desperately in need of and biologically inclined for. We rob ourselves of our genetic human birthright - to be meaningfully coupled and paired, surrounded by our loving and caring children and family.

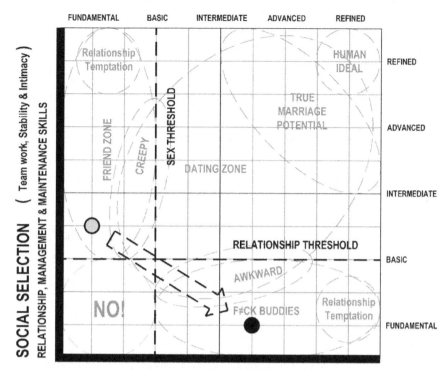

FUNDAMENTAL   BASIC   INTERMEDIATE   ADVANCED   REFINED

Relationship Temptation

HUMAN IDEAL — REFINED

TRUE MARRIAGE POTENTIAL — ADVANCED

FRIEND ZONE

CREEPY

SEX THRESHOLD

DATING ZONE — INTERMEDIATE

RELATIONSHIP THRESHOLD — BASIC

AWKWARD

NO!

F#CK BUDDIES

Relationship Temptation — FUNDAMENTAL

SOCIAL SELECTION (Team work, Stability & Intimacy)
RELATIONSHIP, MANAGEMENT & MAINTENANCE SKILLS

NATURAL SELECTION (Survival, Seduction & Provision)
PHYSICAL, SEXUAL & SOCIAL DISPLAY DIMORPHISMS

Common Failures: The PUA (Pick Up Artist) Promise

All marketers know and we naturally understand that sex sells. Sex sells to our biologically driven needs and sexual cues, as well as our socially engrained social cues as well. When coupled with entertainment it has created a platform for human consumption massive in scale. We are surrounded by it. We've come to expect it and feel left lacking when not stimulated by these impulses, and in the world of sex and entertainment there are only a few things that surpass this combination; illicit/taboo sex and aspirational sex. Sex that either focuses on forbidden association and practices and those that are characterized by a desire for social prestige and validation that comes with sexual success. Professional pick up artists (PUAs) and the companies they've established are providing content,

The MAP- A Personal Guide to the Sexual Marketplace

coaching, training and community forums that combine all of these elements of enticement and intrigue that promise to provide all of that.

This is an industry the scale of which is made possible by the digital age. It has enabled individuals to create and foster shared information (content), to market and distribute it and to coalesce a shared social environment between individuals while being simultaneously disdained and scorned upon culturally. For an individual who is ill-prepared or who lacks sexual fluency they are culturally placed in a purgatory of sorts where those that are prepared and sexually fluent are rewarded, but if they attempt to openly gain this knowledge they are culturally scorned, mocked and ridiculed. In effect they are doubly excluded. The result for individuals lacking these abilities is a form of social/sexual alienation and isolation that compounds the distress and strain of their lives, to which some of the PUA industry thrives on and exploits.

At its core this is an industry created by the failures, dysfunctions and voids found within modern western society. In the cultural diminishment of men, it attempts to play the critical role fathers play within society and toxic inequalities of modern feminism.

Against this back drop are two strains of men who are trying to become men women value, expect and ultimately choose: those that are actively making attempts to rise above this cultural and social tide and those that learning to swim within it, reaping wholesale benefits of social collapse.

The fundamental underpinnings of the pickup industry is that they are fulfilling a social void by providing young men who have not received it a base line education in socio-sexual male-female dynamic, the socio-sexual skills development and training required for it, and a community outlet that fosters a camaraderie and a newfound purpose and place within society. The services offered by pick up artists are precisely ones that society on a whole and women expect young men to "naturally" undergo and reward when they do, but are highly skeptical, hostile and condemning when taught formally and openly to young men who are awkward or not as socially capable as their peers. These are men who are plowed under by a culture and society that expects them to manifest these traits and abilities through osmosis in the absence of instruction or guidance from missing fathers or masculine role models, while transitioning through an already chaotic and stressful adolescence. This is the social and cultural framework from which a social sexual industry has emerged in responding to a growing demand as society and culture fails more and more men.

The essence of what the pickup industry promises is to teach and refine those skills, attributes and abilities that will move someone that's stuck in the Friend Zone out of it and into a sexually heroic and sustained bachelorhood lifestyle. A world of free and readily available sex with no commitment, no obligation, low investment and limited financial outlay - and that world and reality actually does exist, but it doesn't happen often! Early practitioners would sell their services to individuals that were desperately trying to change their lives and sexual self-identity to match those that were culturally celebrated and rewarded - bad boys. They were taught to mimic "Alpha" males (male pack leadership traits and behaviors) by highly amplifying their physical and social presence, behaving in socially physical and sexually dominant ways and then getting sexually aggressive. Now, to be fair, these traits do work. They actually do. But not for people who are not dialed in physically, socially or sexually, and particularly when these skill sets are all well beyond an individual's zone of proximal development. When massive leaps like this are conducted they usually end up in spectacular failures and wrecks with accompanying fallout.

We can see a number of results like this when we analyze the path taken from the Friend Zone to the Fuck Buddy Zone as marketed by PUAs (Review the graph for detail visual depiction of the path we'll be discussing). Initially, the vast majority of the information and concepts presented to someone who's been dismissed sexually and socially will be overwhelming and subtle comprehension of application will be utterly lost, because

The MAP- A Personal Guide to the Sexual Marketplace

individuals in the Friend Zone have actively rejected or resisted and thus manifested their placement in the Friend Zone. It is also incredibly frightening to try something new, let alone so out of your own reality. Hesitancy, apprehension and suspicion are common and should be expected. As such, individuals will not normally embrace all of the teachings of PUAs, but they will shift their social position from being dismissed to being known. Unfortunately, they will now have moved into the realm of being Creepy after displaying incredible courage and fortitude to get there. They display physical postures, social behaviors and sexual aggressiveness that they are not congruent with, and this will be telegraphed to their social audience and will come across as socially and sexually creepy, which result in failure; both personal and sexual rejection from their target audience. These social and sexual rejections are brutal to the uninitiated. They're hard to the initiated. At this point, many people simply quit and give up with accompanying resentment for having even attempted it. Others persevere and lean into the process with hope, faith and peer support.

>*note to those who have attempted this self-transformation based upon this path; perhaps your intentions were right and just, but the path and expectations you took and held were terribly wrong. All failures beg for introspection. Let your failures lead to introspection and refinement, not rejection and cessation. How different could have your results been had you first attempted to move your Natural Selection traits into the 'Average' zone and then learned the skills and traits associated with remaining single, equating that to being in the 'Fuck Buddy Zone'. You would still face rejection, but it would be from people worth being rejected by, not those of a grossly unpalatable disposition and nature.

Individuals who have a measure of success will find themselves in a unique space for the first time; the Dating Zone. They've managed to get near or just beyond the sexual threshold to become someone's viable (situationally) sexual option. The problem is that this area is at the bottom of the Dating Zone pool. These are individuals who are below average in sexual appeal and below average socially (not your best options for sustained happiness or fulfillment). As a result, the relationship attempts that spring from this area are doomed to failure from the start as they entice little to no investment due to their low sexual values and are not sustainable because the parties involved simply lack the social ability to sustain them. Sadly, for those individuals who were previously dismissed, this area of life may seem the best they can afford themselves. They have not experience better, have such low self-esteem and worth due to their life narrative and lack a support group that will coax them into continuing their journey of self-development and better more appropriate relationship partner selection. People who enter into subpar relationships with recognizably subpar attributes, abilities and skills are doing so out of a driven need for fulfillment, as they are not self-functioning innately. They have a driven and dependent need on others. This is the realm ripe with a host of dysfunctional social orders and relationship structures in the loss of self, evolving into co-dependency, failures in communication, lack of healthy boundary setting, imbalance and high reactivity and compulsivity, all coupled with an inability to appropriately weigh the consequences of one's decisions. External solutions in the form of relationships with others will not solve internal issues unrecognized or attended to.

Those individuals that make it further along the pickup artist pathway and progression will suddenly reach the Awkward Zone. Here, individual as well as cultural factors begin to create considerable tension and complexity that the aspiring PUA is not well suited to handle, frequently resulting in less than marginal results and utter disasters. The mantra and refrain for those in this position that keep cycling sexual partner failure after sexual partner failures due to the pressures and tensions associated with relationship potentiality is simply to wash, rise and repeat; simply go out and bang ten other people to develop the emotional insensitivity to the failure. In essence, this process is consciously developing and with specific intent antisocial or sociopathic attitudes, beliefs and behaviors with regard to sex and intimacy.

Those that actually manage to achieve PUA nirvana have consciously developed anti-social traits and behaviors associated with gross disregard for the feelings of others, a lack of shame or remorse for behavior and unchecked manipulative behavior to meet their sexual needs. In many ways, they will openly broadcast these traits and strangely enough this will actually serve as an attractant to interested parties, but as time will continue to attest, people who end up here are either grossly emotionally and psychologically disturbed already, or will become so in short order with the as expected emotional and psychological breakdown that comes from being emotionally and psychologically ostracized. There is a marked difference in the ambition to become someone of high social value and remain single in pro-social way (which demands honesty, agency and accountability for all parties), as opposed to the "get laid at nearly any cost" approach that many PUAs manifest.

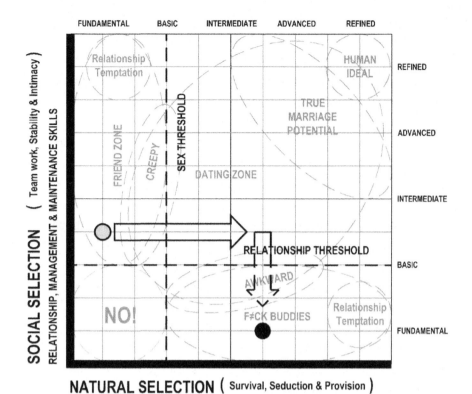

SOCIAL SELECTION (Team work, Stability & Intimacy)
RELATIONSHIP, MANAGEMENT & MAINTENANCE SKILLS

Relationship Temptation

FRIEND ZONE

CREEPY

SEX THRESHOLD

HUMAN IDEAL — REFINED

TRUE MARRIAGE POTENTIAL — ADVANCED

DATING ZONE — INTERMEDIATE

RELATIONSHIP THRESHOLD — BASIC

AWKWARD

NO!

F#CK BUDDIES   Relationship Temptation — FUNDAMENTAL

NATURAL SELECTION (Survival, Seduction & Provision)
PHYSICAL, SEXUAL & SOCIAL DISPLAY DIMORPHISMS

There is a secondary path, and one that the industry has more and more shifted to as the failure and blow-back from such failures adversely affected individual's business and their reputation within the industry. It is one in which was initially embraced by those that had greater social advantages in the form of education, profession and personal reputation not to mention age and maturity than their younger colleges in learning the skills and craft of womanizing. Given this differential in starting position they held considerable hesitancy, apprehension and suspicions to over-the-top exhibition, social displays and behaviors promoted by these companies which lead them to avoid such behaviors, but to embrace and accept social-normalized behaviors that advance their sexual market value appreciably without being obviously counter-cultural. Due to this, they not only dramatically changed their sexual worth they were well within the Dating

Zone and were socializing with individuals above the relationship threshold sufficiently avoiding the Awkward Zone completely. In due course, these individuals eventually disappeared from the pick up community because they either removed those negative traits or lack of abilities that kept them from success and became sufficiently self-sufficient or they created opportunities with potential partners and entered into relationships. If those relationships failed, often they would return, but again only to leave once more due to finding another relationship, by re-applying previously learned skill sets to attain self-sufficiency and group independence.

For the most part most of the companies today actually do and are capable of providing services that lead to sustained bachelorhood for individuals that have raised their sexual values and become socially and sexually congruent with both. The truth is this is not only evermore feasible, but culturally incentivized. People have successfully transformed their social and sexual lives and in that process, to a degree I believe, they have achieved what they set out to achieve, but I don't think it's ultimately sustainable or beneficial to society on a whole. As a species, we are meant to be social animals by our very nature of being mammals. It is a biological reality that has real world consequences when ignored; we are deeply unhappy, sexually unfulfilled and genetically we become a dead end or limited contributor to the human population. Mankind has thrived where families and family unity have been strong and in that absence, we see social, moral and material decay.

The abilities and skills to be social and sexual are essential to individual potential of fulfillment, as well as the good of society particularly when they are guided and channeled toward social creation (families) rather than social destruction, as we are currently seeing in the form of social narcissism and denial epidemic. We should be cognizant of the critical role sex, sexual identity/role and family or the lack of one and spills out in the life of the dysfunctional. Individuals terribly frustrated by their own awkwardness and inabilities who then seek to compensate for it, much of it socially induced and supported stubborn immaturity wedded to towering narcissism that perpetuates adolescence for both men and women, free from the constraints and obligations associated with the responsibilities and demands of civilized adulthood in the form of childrearing. This is a cultural and social failure to promote individuals to mature out of social confusion and a preparedness to assume the mantle of parenthood, which is the historically successful bulwark against social and societal chaos. We naturally don't want to face these realities because it challenges our social, cultural and political narratives we've grown to accept and expect particularly where biological reality and social constructs are concerned.

A sea change in social attitudes needs to occur where social held values channel men and women toward creation and sustainment, rather than destruction and demise.

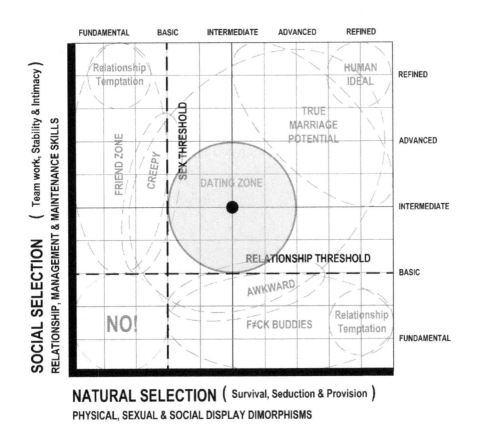

SOCIAL SELECTION (Team work, Stability & Intimacy)
RELATIONSHIP, MANAGEMENT & MAINTENANCE SKILLS

FUNDAMENTAL   BASIC   INTERMEDIATE   ADVANCED   REFINED

Relationship Temptation

FRIEND ZONE

CREEPY

SEX THRESHOLD

DATING ZONE

HUMAN IDEAL   REFINED

TRUE MARRIAGE POTENTIAL   ADVANCED

INTERMEDIATE

RELATIONSHIP THRESHOLD   BASIC

AWKWARD

NO!   F#CK BUDDIES   Relationship Temptation   FUNDAMENTAL

NATURAL SELECTION (Survival, Seduction & Provision)
PHYSICAL, SEXUAL & SOCIAL DISPLAY DIMORPHISMS

DATING ZONE

Welcome to the Dating Zone; the home of normal and average.

Up to now, we have been observing and evaluating two zones where individuals have serious problems understanding, comprehending, and appropriately comport themselves within the sexual marketplace to garner the results they desire; those in the Friend or Fuck Buddy

The MAP- A Personal Guide to the Sexual Marketplace

Zones. In either case, they fail to cross a significant threshold in order to turn themselves into viable mates and partners. With this chapter, we will be investigating the center of our map and what it means for each gender to be squarely within the Dating Zone for partnering and mate selection.

Before we do so, congratulations is in order for those modifying their lives, behaviors and outlooks to get to this point. Self-reconstruction is an art form and they have achieved that, putting the hard, disciplined work in to achieve this. Too often we focus on the difficulties endured to our achievements, but rarely do we observe and take note from the views from where we now stand. Take that time and appreciate the positive benefits and changes to your life. The big. The small. The joyful. Those are yours. You earned them. You made them manifest. Own them, as they are yours, and carry them with pride.

The second order before we begin is the place in which a third-group will be now joining us. Those individuals who are starting out both above the sex threshold and relationship threshold, who are likely just haven't put all the pieces together, as to how and why the sexual marketplace is the way that it is, and how they fit into it. They are undoubtedly having difficulty navigating this environment, and why shouldn't they as it is something they just don't quite comprehend to have and live the life that they feel should be theirs. And they are right in believing so. They should be entitled to healthy, loving, intimate relationships, but something just isn't measuring up. To those readers who have read the first two chapters and are jumping ahead to this point as it is the most likely appropriately category for them, I welcome you all.

For this discussion, we will be looking at the consequences and implications of having your sexual market score (average Social Selection score & Natural Selection score) that falls within the central portion of the Sexual Marketplace Map. By all accounts this means your scores/ratings are perfectly normal and average. In fact, based on the complexity level of these categories they average out to an intermediate level for both Social and Natural Selection. Most people, men and women live here... by definition. It's called being normal. It's called being average.

The Nature of Average

The problems with "normal" and "average" is it isn't the safe, albeit comfortable place we've come to believe it to be. The reality about being "normal" or "average" is that there are significant dangers and risks associated with either being or achieving "normal" or "average". In the two previously discussed zones, both are personal hells. They are the zones in which people are tormented, tortured and ostracized. The middle may seem safe, but it isn't, because everything here is at risk. From getting too comfortable, from getting worn down and your results start to slip, or simply by being out competed and over-run by your betters. The results and determination of these repeated semi-failures just hasn't been delivered yet. They are delayed, but the bill will still come due. Even if you do manage to sustain a life time of balancing being "normal" or "average" it is a constant struggle just to do so. It is a life constantly teetering on failure, yet shying away from actual success. It's a life consigned to the limbo of not knowing.

Furthermore, the middle/normal/average is where people naturally want to relax and take a break. That's normal and should happen to consolidate resources, regain strength, energy and the resolve to carry on. It should be a "break", not a "stopping" point. Too often though it isn't even a stopping point, but the aiming point for far too many people, who desire for more, but are unwilling to endure discomfort to seek the gains and advantages that they need and want in life.

Let's take a closer look at "Average", particularly when we view ourselves, how we view others, and how others view us and the nature of our relationships:

Is "Average" certain?

Is "Average" in control?

Is "Average" managed?

If you were "Certain, in Control and Managed", you wouldn't be "Average". You would be Extraordinary.

If others viewed you as "Certain, in Control and Managed", others wouldn't consider you "Average". They would consider you Extraordinary.

If your employer or customers viewed you as "Certain, in Control and Managed" they wouldn't consider you "Average". They would consider you Extraordinary.

If your relationship was "Certain, in Control and Managed", your relationships wouldn't be "Average". They would be Extraordinary.

How do you now view "Average" when evaluated this way?

Another way of looking at this is from your perspective:

How attractive to you is the uncertainty of "Average"?

How safe to you is the lack of control of "Average"?

What do you think are the benefits and rewards for unmanaged of "Average"?

Would you want to be sold a product or service that is "Average"? A product or service that comes with uncertainty, lack of safety, and questionable return of investment? Would you want to sell a product or service that is "Average"?

I ask, because if you are "Average", that is you. That is you in the sexual marketplace. You're doing just enough to be a potential value while at the same time doing the least enough not to get fired or replaced. You're doing what most people do, what most people expect and therefore there's no breaking out of the crowd for you to distinguish yourself as the better option. The problem with "average" or "normal" is that it is unremarkable. There's nothing special about it. Nothing worthy of notice or remark. You are just as good as your peers and thus forgettable. As an individual, you just don't stand out. You didn't overcome the resistance, pressure or have the discipline to be extra-ordinary.

Let's talk about your dreams for a little bit. Do you want your dreams to remain figments of your imagination or would you actually want them materialized? Are dreams and ambitions really dreams and ambitions when they can be commonly had? When "Average" can achieve them? Of course not. Dreams are never achieved by being "Average". Extraordinary things just don't happen when knowledge, thinking and actions are ordinary. That is unless you have "Faith", which is holding a belief despite the presence of evidence and reason, or the law of averages just doesn't apply to you because you're special. Here's a hint: you're not.

AVERAGE IS AT RISK...

The reality about "Average" is that everything about average is at risk and so despite escaping the Friend/Awkward zones, the results are mediocre.

> If you are "Average" in appearance, demeanor and social skills; your partnership attraction ability will be mediocre. In today's sexual marketplace, if you are "Average", you just don't exist as an option of choice. Nobody willingly commits to "Average" over something that's obviously is "better than Average".

> "Average" job? your satisfaction, income, benefits and options derived from those in life are all going to be mediocre. Economically it's called the Middle Class but could have just as well been called the "Average Class".

> If your marriage is "Average", it will be mediocre as a result. Tell me about the qualitative experiences you think you'll have in an

The MAP- A Personal Guide to the Sexual Marketplace

"Average" marriage. What do you think the real results will actually be?

If you are average as a parent, your children will be mediocre as a result as well. Children thrive with active parenting. What do you think the result of "Average" parenting will be for your children? "Whatever, it's good enough..." For you children? For your legacy? For the only thing that will likely survive you, "Average" is sufficient?

If your life is "Average", you will live a mediocre existence. How do you think this will end for you?

Average is a Low Investment Driver

Average doesn't drive investment. People naturally want a beneficial return on any investment, whether that be time, energy, resources or emotions. We intuitively know that when we invest in average that the results will be-average/mediocre. As such, "Average" isn't valued. Furthermore, it is in such high supply that it's a cheap commodity to begin with. Making the sale of "Average" will be done due to randomness, frustration, exacerbation or a combination of each those in the buyer. It's called settling.

Where previously we looked at the results of "Average", let's put it in the context how others view us as "Average";

Our job and employer - how likely is it that they are going to value "Average"? Is your job "Certain"? Your performance isn't "Certain" when it's average. How likely are they to replace you with someone who's likely to outperform you or comes at a lower cost? In a good economy this is a potentiality, as businesses strive for competitiveness. In a poor economy, how "Certain" are you that you won't be laid off? If your company is struggling, are you an asset or a deficit? You're neither and that doesn't help them, or you.

The MAP- A Personal Guide to the Sexual Marketplace

Your target market within the SMP - how likely is it that he or she is going to be interested in "Average"? Is this something that they are going to be willing to go out of their way to engage, nurture or pursue? Nope. You're a face that makes up the crowd.

How about your relationship? Is your partner going to be willing to invest time, energy and to dedicate themselves to a relationship that is "Average"? How about upkeeping themselves? How inclined is your partner going to be to maintain themselves, their sensuality and sexuality when you're proffering "Average"? Nobody says, "Hell yeah!" to "Average", when there are so many offerings that exceed your own.

Just because you're married, doesn't mean that Hypergamy and Hypogamy rest. Want to create regret and doubt in a marriage? Offer up "Average" in the relationship, at home and in the marriage. Our biological nature doesn't rest and marriage is no safe refuge from Hypergamy and Hypogamy. They are either satiated by providing "Certainty", "Control" and "Management" or they are not. If not, you are relying on relationship equity, faith and social constructs to secure your marriage. Good luck, because you're playing with biological fire. In today's cultural environment, that is beyond naive and terribly foolish because nature is unrelenting.

Average is diminished by the extraordinary

Another problem with "Average" is that it is diminished by everything greater than it in contrast, which honestly will be quite a bit. When you, your job, your relationship, your marriage and life are not "certain, in control and managed" you will be and feel diminished by everything greater. That's no way to be. That's not way to love. That's no way to commit and that is no way to live.

The general reason that the extraordinary diminishes average isn't because extraordinary is better. It's because it's MUCH better. The rewards and benefits for being extraordinary are not proportional to the additional work. The problem is that on the path to get to extraordinary there is a long period where the result is diminished or marginal in comparison to the gain. It's not an even a simple progression line. Because of that, not everyone is willing to put in the hard effort to become better educated about relationship skills, management abilities, or maintenance protocols to better themselves or their relationships. Furthermore, not everyone is willing to go through the tough conversations, hurt feelings, risks of being rejected and psychological drama required to better their relationships. To get to the payoff where time, energy, and resources are reaping significant rewards you have to push through this performance plateau and endure regular exercise and discipline of your skills to achieve the results you want. It is human nature to want to quit or to back off when things get difficult and yet it is this behavior that creates the scarcity of the extraordinary. When people hit this plateau of performance they often give up. When repeated enough, you develop the patterns of a quitter. To break out of "Average" we will need to be prepared to resist this urge to quit, to fold to difficulties, to succumb to resistance of progress. If we are not, it begs the very real question; should you have even gone down this path?

Average Sucks!

This should come as no surprise at this point. Average doesn't usually work long-term. Any undertaking that incudes average ideas or actions will likely fail you sooner or later. Any activity conducted at average levels will simply not get the job done. Striving for average is just treading water... it's only a matter of time before you fail, because you've lost your purpose and without a purpose you lose motivation. Without those two things, you're just paying the bills, working a job, punching a clock and going through the motions in a relationship and in life.

The MAP- A Personal Guide to the Sexual Marketplace

To put it into context of "Average" in dating, relationship, marriage and childrearing today, consider these statistics:

- 25% of Millennials will never marry, when the clear majority of them have stated a preference to in recent polling.

- 50% divorce threshold for marriages today.
    - 41% of first marriages end in divorce. Less than 12% thought divorce was a potentiality going into the marriage.
    - 60% of second marriages end in divorce.
    - 90% of third marriages end in divorce. Alternating partners doesn't change the equation.

- Child Poverty is almost exclusively a resultant of failed relationships & marriages.
    - 41% of single mother households fall below the poverty line, as compared to 22% of single fathers and 9% of married families.

- Divorce is incredibly detrimental to children and corresponds to the following factors:
    - 90% of homeless children
    - 85% of behavioral disorders
    - 75% of Substance Abuse
    - 71% pregnant teenagers
    - 71% of High School Drop Outs

    The stats here could go on and on.

When we let go of our sense of agency, purpose and investment into the underlying elements of success, the consequences are dire for all involved. When we don't, the outcomes are simply extraordinary in comparison.

You must be aware of the high cost of low living, by cheap thinking and of embracing "Average" as be good enough. As soon as you begin to exceed average in your thinking, approach and decisions, you will immediately start influencing other areas of your life. We intuitively know that "Average" is the home for long-term regret and doubt... which is why there is so little desire to invest in "Average". Doubly, it is an acknowledgment that we couldn't afford better for ourselves and we settled. It is this paring that makes accepting "Average" such a caustic pill to swallow.

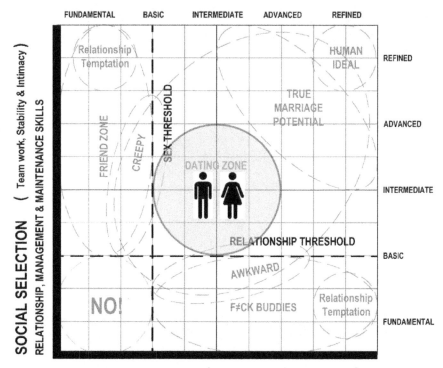

Culture & Society Matter

Culture and Society influence individual perceptions and create the framework for what is socially acceptable from the private sphere to the public sphere. It is however terribly important to remember that these constructs have a basis originating and emanating from our biological imperatives; Natural Sexual Selection. In humans, these sexual biological imperatives are clustered into categories of physical and social behavioral expressions related to sexual selection. We have previously defined them as Survival dimorphisms (prerequisites to evolutionary survival), Seduction dimorphisms (leading to procreation) and Provision dimorphisms (social survival provisionary traits). Where men and women are the same, the dimorphisms are very similar. Where we differ, they diverge and take sex

The MAP- A Personal Guide to the Sexual Marketplace

specific specialization. For women, this gender specific imperative is known as Hypergamy and for men it's known as Hypogamy. This cluster of biological imperatives will drive behavior, selection and desire when exhibited by the opposite sex. In turn, the individual must trigger similar responses in significant and consistent quantity to attract and secure a partner.

Furthermore, we must also take into account that nature is amoral. Nature doesn't have a conscience. Nor is it concerned about ethics. Nature is a result orientated system. Survival of the fittest. As such, the means & methods are discretionary to the achievement of biological species success. Quite often, these means and methods would be what we currently call Machiavellian, sociopathic, narcissistic, solipsistic, etc., i.e. "by any means necessary", is fair game in nature.

Unconstrained, Nature and thus the elements of Natural Sexual Selection are opportunistic for both sexes, whether that be for survival, seduction or provision. Simply put, Nature doesn't care how you get your business on, just that you do. By evolution each sex adapted to the particular challenges, both in Nature and an opposing opportunistic gender strategy that confronted them, which has led to some very interesting and fascinating counter sexual response dynamics. Often these too ended up getting imprinted into our human genome, as a response to successful breeding adaptations (those that failed didn't breed and thus currently don't have a say in our genetics. Only the successful/survivors do). Other responses have been codified and passed on socially and culturally to constrain, guide, control or conceal our base biological impulses, so that we may be able to live and survive in ever greater human clusters and colonies, which we ultimately define as Societies and Civilizations. As a species, we have leveraged Society and Cultures, as constructs, in order to provide 'Certainty, Control and Management' to our environmental and social conditions for our species success.

I think it's important at this point to take a step back and recognize that our base biological natures (Hypergamy and Hypogamy) are meant and have proven to be compatible with each other _when naturally ordered_. We're evolved to be, in order to promote human survival & thriving. It is precisely how we are geared. It is when we are imbalanced, that we individually and collectively face significant issues and challenges that tax and stress our social constructs, which we are seeing today.

Because we are a sex-based species we will need to look, based on gender at the Dating Zone and see how culture & society influences the gender dynamics within the sexual marketplace for each. Social norms are explicit or implicit rules that define expectation of what is appropriate behavior within society and will guide the gender norms. The gender norms are a subset to this that are sex specific and can commonly be referred to as gender stereo-types within either masculinity or femininity and will guide individual behavioral expression.

Female Cultural & Social Expectations (Hypergamy)

Traditional female social expectations for women generally tended toward women being more passive, nurturing and supporting socially and relative to men. Ultimately women were expected to become wife, then matriarch of the home and family life, providing essential primary care, family and household management as part of her societal expectations.

As a product of the cultural shift spearheaded by the second wave of feminism, women have been increasingly expected to be educated, worldly and have fulfilling professional careers, while taking ever shorter, short-term maternity leaves prior to returning to work and out sourcing much of the daily care, support & supervision of her children to lower hourly paid child-care personnel, with no anticipated appreciable degradation in value to child, home or spouse due to her inevitable unavailability. While the radical feminists have seen domestication and child rearing as an aberration, the feminist ideal notion that a woman can have and do it all, has cascaded through the generations to a point socially that women are deeply torn between having a career, contributing to the household or being a primary care giver to her children and family.

Currently women are also discovering and seeing first hand that the pressures and dynamics of professional life and the anticipated external validation associated with a career outside of the home, particularly when coupled with responsible parenthood, are not measuring up to what was advertised and promoted. Furthermore, they are laying witness to the human carnage and tragedy associated with failed marriages, failed families and failed lives. There is an underlying tension and anxiety for women who have been guided culturally between ambition and political ideology in forgoing children for career. They cannot un-see the hollowness associated with the lives of these sexual refugees, who have failed at both; career and children and their biological imperative toward domesticity, and then go on to celebrate the ruin of their lives and lying about it in louder and louder voices... They can see it, if not intuitively sense the human tragedy that started with all the promise as their own. Refugees and casualties are not the victors in the game of love or life, they are losers that have lost and everybody knows it. They have been found to be unfit.

It is with these often open and nagging tensions that women enter into the sexual marketplace. Within the sexual marketplace, women's biologic and social expectations have changed remarkably little as there is minimal to no expectation for women to embrace the roles and responsibilities associated with relationship leadership and management associated with initiating social contact (approach & initiate conversation), progressing the socialization (leading the interaction/conversation), advancing and re-initiating social contact (first date follow up), advancing the relationship sexually (seduction and execution), or carrying the burden financially of supporting this socialization. Nearly none of the rites, rituals and obligations associated with courtship, fall within a woman's gender role, responsibility or expectation. She is the prize of the sexual marketplace and she is to be pursued, wooed and competed for.

Furthermore, she is expected and prompted biologically and culturally to seek and discriminate for a partner that has the means and wherewithal to have achieved wealth, status, power and fame. In simpler terms, she is expected seek a partnership with someone her equal or better, to safeguard her and her future, i.e. marrying up (hypergamy), that best reflects her value in the sexual marketplace.

Male Cultural & Social Expectations (Hypogamy)

Traditional male social expectations generally tended toward men being more assertive, dominant and provisionary, socially and in relative to women. Ultimately men were expected to become husband and then patriarchs of the home and family life; responsible for providing safety, security, being the sole source for resources and competent leadership within the relationship and family.

As a product of the cultural shift spearheaded by the second wave of feminism, men have been increasingly expected to embrace and support the social changes of women in society and the workplace, without noticing or calling attention to its shortcomings or failures, nor benefiting from these social and professional upheavals, which often came at the expense of men, coupled with additional responsibility of agency. As feminism cascaded through the generations, men have progressively lost their place as respected heads of households and honored roles as fathers yet are solely held responsible and hostage for the fulfillment and happiness of those within it or be subject to removal. When radical feminist stated clearly in Marxist terms their desires to "smash the Patriarchy", what part of family values didn't you think they meant? What men didn't they mean?

The catastrophic rise of the second wave of feminism and the hyper-inflation of the welfare state allowed for the break down and destruction of the family structure by removing women's need for virtuous men, to be replaced by government subsidies. Women were freed from the shackles

The MAP- A Personal Guide to the Sexual Marketplace

of consequences to a liberated sexuality and with it, virtue within sexual marketplace collapsed. Remember that unconstrained biological imperatives have no morals and is opportunistic and because of this there was no need or incentive to discriminate for partners that showcased and exemplified the qualities that lead to protection, provision and the raising of children; the State would intervene and provide safeguards to poor decisions made with each. Quite often, actually incentivizing the behaviors through divorce laws and welfare programs.

Increasingly men have also been the target for increasing societal debasement, ridicule and predatorial gender victimization (gynocentrism). As a result, men are increasingly forgoing education, abandoning the workplace and avoiding the maturation process of becoming responsible and capable partners, husbands and fathers, particularly where the benefits and rewards for not doing so have never been greater.

In spite of this, there is an underlying tension and anxiety between this cultural, social and legal reality and men's biological imperative toward and for sexual paring and fathering children. Despite the tremendous social and professional upheavals culturally little has changed in regard to the gender roles associated with agency of courtship; it still primarily resides with men. Nearly all of the rites, rituals and obligations associated with courtship, fall within a man's gender role, responsibility and expectation.

Furthermore, he is expected and prompted biologically and culturally to seek and discriminate for a partner that he has the means and wherewithal to protect, provide for and raise a family with. In simpler terms he is to over produce (a requirement for provision of others) and is disposable (his security is second to his partner's and his family). In most cases this mean partnering with and marrying a woman at or below his station in life, i.e. marrying down.

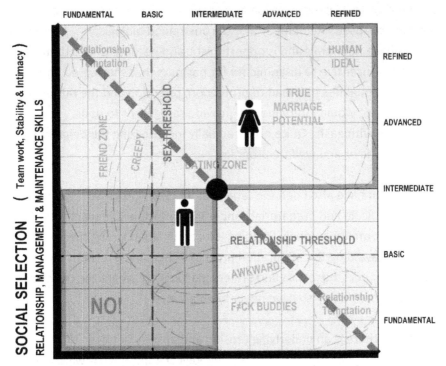

FUNDAMENTAL   BASIC   INTERMEDIATE   ADVANCED   REFINED

SOCIAL SELECTION (Team work, Stability & Intimacy)
RELATIONSHIP, MANAGEMENT & MAINTENANCE SKILLS

Relationship Temptation   HUMAN IDEAL   REFINED

TRUE MARRIAGE POTENTIAL   ADVANCED

FRIEND ZONE   CREEPY   SEX THRESHOLD   DATING ZONE   INTERMEDIATE

RELATIONSHIP THRESHOLD   BASIC

AWKWARD

NO!   F#CK BUDDIES   Relationship Temptation   FUNDAMENTAL

NATURAL SELECTION (Survival, Seduction & Provision)
PHYSICAL, SEXUAL & SOCIAL DISPLAY DIMORPHISMS

Dating Zone: Gender & Cultural Options

Having discussed male and female cultural and social expectations when it comes to the sexual marketplace individually, let's again place them together, with an overlay of what those cultural and social expectations imply for equally scored male and female in the sexual marketplace.

At first observation there is tremendous range and opportunity for choice for the average woman; 3/4 of the entire sexual marketplace with her prime zone for selection being those males that exceed average in both the Natural Selection traits of survival, seduction & provision and Social Selection traits of team work, stability and intimacy. In short, all of her primary choices are extraordinary. Furthermore, the advantages for

The MAP- A Personal Guide to the Sexual Marketplace

securing a partner in this category offer tremendous advantages not only for a woman's station in life, but the qualitative nature of it, as the majority of her choices will lie above the 50% divorce threshold. She will simply live a far better life for doing so, because her partner is so far more capable socially and sexually to meet her expectations and represents something that she's more likely to invest in, maintain and repair should strife or hardship arise, which they will.

The average male on the other hand has remarkably fewer options with over 1/4 of those being in an absolute 'No-Go!' territory. Worse yet, nearly 86% of his options fall below the sex threshold or below the relationship threshold, leaving a scant 16% that's within the 'datable range'. Worse of all, is that ALL of his options are below average, even the 16% in the 'datable range' fall below the average mark in Sexual and Social Selection. That means ALL of his options are sub-ordinary and below the relative 50% divorce threshold. For all that, he is expected to over-produce, protect and committedly raise a family with a sub-par woman, monogamously (she holds a sexual monopoly). Consequently, his life will be greatly diminished and at risk for significant failures for making such a decision and commitment.

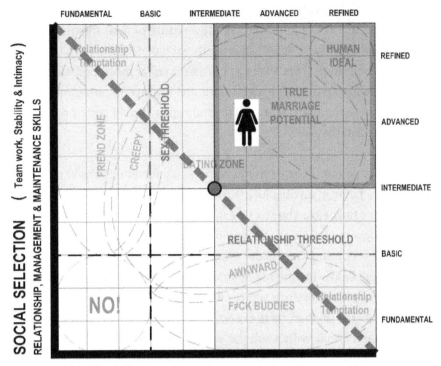

Chart labels:
- Top axis: FUNDAMENTAL, BASIC, INTERMEDIATE, ADVANCED, REFINED
- Right axis: REFINED, ADVANCED, INTERMEDIATE, BASIC, FUNDAMENTAL
- Left axis: SOCIAL SELECTION (Team work, Stability & Intimacy) — RELATIONSHIP, MANAGEMENT & MAINTENANCE SKILLS
- Within chart: Relationship Temptation, HUMAN IDEAL, FRIEND ZONE, CREEPY, SEX THRESHOLD, TRUE MARRIAGE POTENTIAL, DATING ZONE, RELATIONSHIP THRESHOLD, AWKWARD, NO!, F#CK BUDDIES, Relationship Temptation

NATURAL SELECTION (Survival, Seduction & Provision)
PHYSICAL, SEXUAL & SOCIAL DISPLAY DIMORPHISMS

DATING ZONE- FEMALE PERSPECTIVE

As we touched on in the previous section, women on a whole are expected and prompted biologically and culturally to seek and discriminate for a partner that arouses her interests sexually which are the Natural Selection traits of Survival & Seduction traits (physical stature, health, fitness, deliberate sexual enticement, provocation & execution) and meets or exceeds her selection criteria of Provision based on wealth, status, power and fame to safe guard her future, all of which is colloquially referred to as "marrying up". Her success in doing so reflects her value in the sexual marketplace.

When we observe this graphically, we can observe that an average woman commands a very wide range of variation and choice of potential partners.

The MAP- A Personal Guide to the Sexual Marketplace

In our Map she commands a range of ¾ of the entire Sexual Marketplace, with all of her choices being 'above average' in the realms of Natural Selection; physical & sexual attraction, as well as the ability to provide. Her choices are also 'above average' in the Social Selection range, where we can expect her partners to be 'above average' in the following abilities; team work (relationship skills), stability (managements) and Intimacy (maintenance). The advantages for securing a partner at or above her abilities offer tremendous advantages not only in her life situationally, but also with regard to the qualitative nature of it, as her partner is better suited and prepared to ensure the thriving of the relationship both socially and sexually. This is particularly important when we consider that most marriages, approximately 50%, will end up in divorce. Having a partner that is "above average" means that she is more likely to invest back into the relationship, maintain and repair it should strife or hardship arise, and have a partner in hand who has greater than average ability to do the same and to work things through appropriately.

It's worth noting at this point that most "average women" who are serially unable to acquire a suitable partner and are unhappy about this, are not being choosy or having higher standards, they're just not worth doing business with. Meaning that they're actually not average, but below average, but rate themselves higher. This is rather typical for everyone. The problem is the sexual marketplace is clearly telling them something based on the results they're achieving. There could be several reasons for this; a lack of knowledge, understanding, their positioning within the physical SMP, marketing, branding of etc... or they're are most likely embracing and clearly telegraphing a form of socio-political-gender ideology (feminism) that simply warns quality men to appropriately avoid any contact and connection with them other than purely being social. When women think they are broadcasting a "strong, independent, pro-feminist view" they don't come across in a positive manner to relationship centric men who know better. They may feel like they are symbolically a "fire truck" attending to the disasters of social injustices, but in reality far too many men are symbolically seeing them as the "ambulance" and nobody is looking to go on that ride. Unfortunately, in this regard too many of the "should be average" women are simply too horrid to actually consider dealing with past some fucking. I actually doubt any of my readers are truly in this last category because it wouldn't become those who are to pick a book up like this, actually read it and get something out of it. That would require introspection, which these women lack and thus determines their results. But, if any of this does resonate with you, please go back and read the chapter on Fuck Buddies, as something is limiting your ability to reap the benefits of being greater than average, or utilize the tremendous innate feminism superpower of empathy and start listening to those good men around you and their fears of the SMP, commitment and women like you.

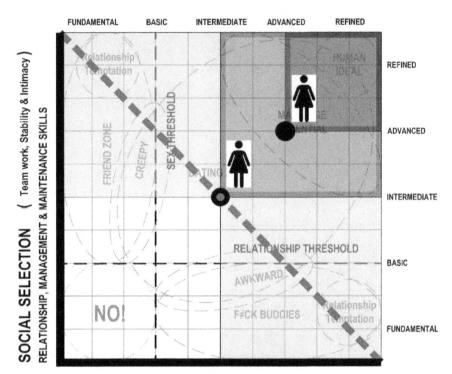

FUNDAMENTAL   BASIC   INTERMEDIATE   ADVANCED   REFINED

SOCIAL SELECTION (Team work, Stability & Intimacy)
RELATIONSHIP, MANAGEMENT & MAINTENANCE SKILLS

REFINED
ADVANCED
INTERMEDIATE
BASIC
FUNDAMENTAL

HUMAN IDEAL

Relationship Temptation

FRIEND ZONE

CREEPY

SEX THRESHOLD

DATING

MARRIAGE POTENTIAL

RELATIONSHIP THRESHOLD

NO!

AWKWARD

F#CK BUDDIES

Relationship Temptation

NATURAL SELECTION (Survival, Seduction & Provision)
PHYSICAL, SEXUAL & SOCIAL DISPLAY DIMORPHISMS

VALUE-TO-OPTION INVERSION

The second incredibly important observation we can make with our SMP Map is that as an "average" woman increases her abilities and SMP value, her options actually ___**DECREASE**___, ...significantly. That's right, when a woman actually works and improves upon herself, she's limiting her options significantly based on her hypergamous nature (desire to seek a better partner). This unfortunately places disproportionate value on higher value males due to competing demands from both "average" and "above average" women who are receptive to either due to their sexual imperative of Hypogamy. It's simply economics. Higher demand + limited product = vastly higher value (purchase cost).

The MAP- A Personal Guide to the Sexual Marketplace

The real problem here isn't that so much of the SMP is currently made up of Natural Selection (naturally), but as a cultural we're not advocating for those solutions that develop and demand high Social Selection traits (marriage, husband, family, fatherhood), and therefore men have been liberated to pursue their own sexual liberation well past middle adulthood, if ever. Yes, Virginia, a ramification of women's sexual revolution is that it too freed the common man to become the players, playboys and badboys that so many of your sisters favor and you're now having to contend with. Not the 1% of men of days ago, but the common dude. Yes, ladies, the radical Marxist feminist have ensured that you are yet one more body they will step over in their march to achieve that "real Marxist utopia" that has failed so many everywhere it has been applied.

What we are left with here is that for women, who are the gate keepers of sex, the only underlying value that is being negotiated with and for, is based on Natural Selection; looks, sexual promiscuity and fertility signals (age). As a culture and as individuals we are not advocating for better. Sure, women want better, but what are they actually DOING about it? How about your choices? What have they been fueled by?

What we're finding is that while the major factor that is being negotiated is Natural Selection Traits (male Hyopogamous interest), women are competing by marketing this (flaunting sexuality and desirability) and under-cutting the high-valued competition, with sexual promiscuity and sexual exploits. It is the driving reasons why a blow-job is the new kiss-good night in the dating realm. Ten years ago, selfies and a sex-tape were the road to celebrity status, which has gone mainstream with reality TV shows and other celebrities leveraging such ventures. What do you think it is today? Why is it so common for a guy to request and receive nude and sexually explicit images from a woman online before they even meet? Honestly, a lot of the time, you don't even have to ask, it's just delivered to keep a guy's attention and focus from the competition. All this goes well beyond the attention seeking sexual validation of sexual enticement online but

The MAP- A Personal Guide to the Sexual Marketplace

physically manifest themselves in the form of tattoos and piercings and into actual sexual predilections that directly mirror men's taste in pornography.

What's worse is that while many decent and often is the case, more mature women refrain from doing so, and cling to their values and ways, they are also being under-cut by ever younger competition who are not only younger, but hotter, fitter (due to their youth) and free of the emotional baggage and value systems to secure the attention of the desirable males who allude you. All of this feeds into male hypogamy, which desires unlimited access to unlimited females, who are young, fit, fertile and sexually adventurous. Just why would a high value male commit to an average woman, when his sexual imperative is being served openly, to his fulfillment, by so many?

Intra-Female Competition

The third element to draw a conclusion from our map is that not only do a woman's options decrease, but her competition level increases proportionally to the decrease in options available. It's an ugly, ugly double-whammy; decreased options and increased competition. These are the primary reasons why women are intersex status seeking and aggressive in relation to their social networks. They have to deal not only with the women within their own circle, but they must contend with the pressures from individuals and groups outside of this social circle. Evolutionary, there was an essential demand that women foster, support and maintain strong connections within their group while still competing for access to vital resources to survive, reproduce and rear young. These actions are typically non-violent, but when pressured, most assuredly were. This plays out with a woman's physical dimorphisms (being smaller & less strong than males) and well as social dimorphisms (being less openly aggressive, more passively/indirectly aggressive than males). In their entirety, women's social network served both supportive and competitive functions which determined her personal and evolutionary success.

Evolutionarily, women had little to gain from competing for numbers of mates, but they have much to gain in terms of securing the highest quality mates and resources for provisioning themselves and their children. Notice the statement read "mates and resources for provisioning", not "mates that provide resources", which is typically what one reads and reads into the situation. This misinterpretation is feeding an industry for the awareness of men into understanding and comprehending that misconception. For men understanding hypergamy is an outreach of nature and mis-reading either is at their peril. It also explains a tremendous amount about the duality of women's sexual nature, and the behavioral patterns that are seen throughout history when resources were scarce, and where stability and dependability were subjective at best.

As is common with both male and females when resources are scarce or difficult to obtain, intrasexual (female-female) aggression increases in frequency and intensity. This Intrasexual aggression is what determines who has the central position within the group and thus access to the prime pick or selection of higher quality foraging areas or mate selections. One of the most important and significant indicators for evolutionary success is a male's ability toward parental care; the ability to protect, provide and raise a family. It is also one of the most studied and recognized benefits a female might obtain from her mate selection. While a single-mother might be able to survive and raise her children alone, we know on a whole they tend to produce low quality offspring and are more likely than not to end up becoming a detriment to society, based on sociology statistics of single-mother households.

In today's environment, we can observe the intra sexual competition of women by viewing women within a given open social environment. Take a dive-bar and swanky lounge, put either woman who identifies with either in the opposing environment and watch the intrasexual display behaviors. Even within the same social class establishment of regular patrons, you will regularly see intrasexual aggressive displays within and between groups, without overt, open aggression. The two primary forms this takes are self-promotion and competitor denigration.

Self-Promotion

With self-promotion women will tend to highlight, flaunt and emphasize their youth, physical attractiveness and sexuality in appearance, dress and behavior displays , both physically or with symbols that reflect status, sexual command and/or social influence. Typically, these symbols are luxury goods and commodities. What and to whom do you think a woman wearing an Alexander Wang cocktail dress, drinking a champagne, holding her Fendi handbag and sporting Louis Vuitton heels is communicating? The assumption used to be that when a woman adorned herself with luxury goods and commodities these were signals to interlopers as to the status and esteem to which HE valued her, due to him having provided her access to those accoutrements. In this regard, it has been noted that the designer handbag or clutch was often a metaphorical shield to fend off and brush off rivals. However, times have clearly changed, and women are providing these commercial commodities for themselves in ever increasing pitch, but WHY? In the Evolutionary Psychology white paper "The Rival Wears Prada: Luxury Consumption as a Female Competition Strategy" Dr De Backer points to the intrasexual competition theory where mate attraction within a given sexual market, triggers a woman's competitive instincts to self-spend on luxuries, as a direct form of self-promotion in terms of broadcast marketing and branding of her SMP value. Studies are proving what we all intuitively embrace, that women who do not consume luxuries are not perceived as attractive or desirable as those who do, who are perceived as being younger, sexier, more attractive, smarter, more mature, worldlier and more successful. It is ostensibly utilized to signal status, social influence and sexual power to provide a barrier to those outside the social network and to center oneself within the network to command relevancy. In this regard, all of the elements associated with femininity and fashion; clothing, make-up, jewelry, and social mannerism and displays are as much for the determent of other women as they are to the benefit of men.

Competitor Denigration

The stigmatizing of female promiscuity aka "Slut Shaming" has often been blamed on men and society, however it is actually utilized and enforced by women to police the sexual undercutting of higher status women. Women used to negotiate with men based on a combination of Natural Selection and Social Selection traits and abilities. Those in combination with sexual scarcity gave women a command advantage within the sexual marketplace. Women who are promiscuous saturate the marketplace with sexual options that were otherwise unavailable and compromise the power-holding position of women as a group and individual high valued status women. In economic terms, when supply increases to meet the demand, the price of a product, service or commodity diminishes. By stigmatizing your competition's reputation, fairly or unfairly, it naturally increases your position by their devaluation with little to no effort, work or dedication to actually improving your value to better compete with theirs. Stigmatizing in this regard is highly effective, as it is a cost efficient strategy to manipulate perceived sexual values and an attempt to maintain sexual value order.

A sister component to stigmatizing competition is the utilization of social exclusion and isolation - the teaming up, or creation of alliances against an interloper or competitor. This form of social behavior is deeply rooted in our evolutionary psyche, where in nature this exclusion and isolation from the group would have made the individual open and vulnerable to attack. In the natural world, this often would have likely meant a death sentence or at a minimum a greatly reduced quality of life and vastly reduced ability to raise and rear children. Even in today's social environment, the signaling of exclusion or isolation from a higher status female toward another, will provide the incentive for other females seeking favor and inclusion within a social network to more aggressively attack the outsider or outcast, in order to curry favorable status with the higher status female. This combination of "mean-girl" stigmatizing, exclusion and isolation isn't limited to "mean little girls" but the whole gamut of intra-female competition and is most prevalent where resources, status, and access and command of high valued men are the greatest. Keep this in mind the next time you see an episode of "House Wives of Beverly Hills" or some other reality show that showcases wives, girlfriends, lovers and baby-mamas of professional athletes. The ugliest stigmatizing takes place not where money is concerned, but power. Observe how women in power handle interlopers; here the veneer of aggression is transparent.

Nasty-Girl

Power, narcissism, sociopathy and Machiavellian behaviors are not well studied, let alone recognized in women, but current research from sexual evolutionary scholars such as Campbell, Cox and Fisher are showing that, much like intra-sexual competition among men, women exhibit or exceeds male capacity for competition within these realms. It is something that society and women on a whole are woefully unwilling to acknowledge, let alone bring attention to. In terms of intra-sexual competition women also have a need to be aware of and defend against the predatory nature of some women. Some women will poach sexual partners, not to replace her as competition for him, but simply to be induced by the elixir of forbidden fruit and the sheer joy of inflicting loss, pain and the heightened drama brought about by grievance from the jilted partner. The longing for something or someone off-limits increases desirability in the human mind and for many, the only thing hotter than hot sex is illicit hot sex. When that sex is either taboo, verboten or dangerous, best yet all three, this drives desire and experience to increasing heights. The male (target) is frequently just a delivery system and a means to an end to achieve this. The clearest sign of a "Nasty-Girl" is that powerful, rebellious, independent, overtly sexual female devoid of a group or network of friends; the shark in the school of fish... or in popular culture vernacular "The Lady in Red", whose own desires for sexual fulfillment are omni important and who relishes in telegraphing it.

Technology

The MAP- A Personal Guide to the Sexual Marketplace

In today's digital culture our social networks have greatly expanded beyond our physical social contact network which has given way to a number of other technologies, services and platforms, which are providing increased means for intra-sexual female competition. Social media in particular has tremendously increased the exposure, marketing and branding efforts of driven incandescent personalities. The ability to self-promote across differing media has never been so powerful in the hands of individuals. Technology has removed the middle-man, the media (entertainment/celebrity journalism), and placed it in the hands of the individual to produce original, scripted content and disseminate that directly to their consumer base. Dating sites have been streamlined down to the essence of Natural Selection in the power of the swipe, either left or right, in seconds limitless options and decisions are made with the swipe of a finger. Others have removed the pretense of romance, virtues and commitment, as prime drivers for social/sexual exchange and have become an ever more increasing "pay for play" proposition, where men of status and means (wealth) can course through a host of females self-promoting their willingness to directly negotiate resources for potential sexual accessibility. Lastly, we should also recognize that intra-sexual female competition is driving the medical and cosmetic surgical industries. Why pay thousands of dollars and dedicate hundreds of hours improving your virtues, when you can jack up your lips, tits and ass to overstimulate male sexual response and place yourself in a sexual desirability class that was beyond your genetics or ability to maintain?

Baby-Mamas

It is a common cliché that beautiful, high status, virtuous women have fewer sex partners than their more common-appearing and aspirational sisters. When you hold social and sexual command virtuously there is little incentive to parse that by casual exchange. High SMP status women can and do capture high SMP status male's attention without leg-spreading enticement. However, women of modest SMP value must exchange attention/opportunity for sexual promiscuity or accept and be consigned to loneliness associated with having not indulged in sex or resign herself to realigning her aims and ambitions to match her sexual selectivity (which todays average women seems extremely reluctant to do). The advantage here is that a high SMP female will have her life filled with deep seated connections of family, friends, deeply held personal values and personal interests that won't compel her, in the same manner as her lesser brethren. However, the lesser female does save out for a singular success, to peak and acquire a high SMP status male's sexual attention, ride that out and then lock down the male's resources with a child. Simply, what you cannot lock down and secure by open enticement of your displayed virtues and values or continue to maintain at sufficient level to sustain commitment, you resort to obligated compliance. Whether that obligated compliance is initiated by a singular opportunity at resource acquisition or via mate-poaching, or I should be clearer, "resource-poaching", it matters only to the extent that the high status male's predisposition or obligated compliance to supply those resources is of concern. In this regard, high status women lose out on potential mates (men) who lack the sexual discipline of discernment and restraint.

HYPOGAMY TRIGGER & SUSTAINMENT FAILURES

The failure of a woman to be able to trigger, command and sustain a man's natural biological sexual selection criteria (hypogamy) will naturally lead to regrettable outcomes:

> **Failure to trigger male hypogamy**: you don't exist as an option sexually or socially.

> **Trigger a males hypogamistic impulse, but not his long-term interests**: you're a sexual option, but not commitment material. A condom is your glass slipper; something you put on for a stranger, but lose by the end of the evening. (see the chapter on 'Fuck buddies' for more detail).

The MAP- A Personal Guide to the Sexual Marketplace

However, failure to maintain the hypogamistic impulse, long or short-term and you'll have a man who is either resigned to obligated compliance or a man who's hypogamistic impulse is seething and building in resentment. Unconstrained hypogamy will seek its fulfillment either appropriately or inappropriately depending upon his options, abilities, means and values. This is the antithesis to natural romantic and poetic order of our beings. This is us succumbing to events, time and a lack of maintenance. It's a run to failure of operation, to which we hope out lasts us, but rarely does, but always consigns us to misery and squalor in the meantime.

New Age Spinsterdom

The mainstreaming of feminism, rise of cultural narcissism and the cultural sustainment of feminine entitlement has given rise to an ever increasing form of involuntary celibacy that is being described as New Age Spinsterdom. Where normally average women have failed to trigger, maintain or sustain masculine long-term hypogamistic interests. The metaphoric description for this is a woman who enjoys the opportunities at seemingly fleeting relationship structure with desirable men, (riding the cock-carousel) which is a seductive and lyrical ride, with exciting ups and downs, until the music and the riding comes to a stop, which typically is preempted by a woman's age, fertility and desirability (hitting the biological wall) to which most if not all of her suitors simply vanish, and her circus comes to a close.

There are some very harsh and unrelenting truths behind the nature of our biology one of which is nature abhors a barren womb. Both biologically in nature and socially. Biologically speaking, time is not endless and a woman's options are made finite both by the physical changes of her body and the passage of time. Her failure to recognize or to act on that is upon her, and her alone. Women can and do rail against this notion, but the reality is your opinion on the subject doesn't matter when it's men's feet that are doing the determining, and if you wait too long, sweetheart, they will walk past you without stopping or acknowledging. This naturally comes as a tremendous shock and is a realization obscured from women by our culture today; that the men that were so plentiful in her youth are simply a disappearing shadow of what her options are today. Women will tell themselves that they are foregoing former sexual promiscuity of yesterday for virtue today by dismissing swarthy sexual suitors, but they are loathe to admit those are the only incoming offers and men they formerly dismissed or currently still would are simply not interested in either an overly aged, worn ride, nor the idea that she was ultimately the best he, after all this time, acquired for himself.

Time is also another increased risk when we take into account that, for anyone living alone for an extended period of time, you may become selfish, self-absorbed and incapable of accommodating the needs of other people, nor have the experience in negotiating through these tensions and conflicts. This coupled with an unrelenting sense of entitlement develops quickly into a situation where the cost of doing business with you exceeds your return worth and value, regardless of what you think or feel about yourself. Again, your opinion doesn't count when it's your potential partner that casts the only vote for investment and commitment.

Cultural Narcissism

It has been said that cultural narcissism is the "new herpes", and not only do you have it, you're willfully pretending that you don't. These statements sting for two reasons: they are injurious to your sense and need for uniqueness ,and its acknowledgment that you are standing in the way of your own happiness and rewards of being loved. Unfortunately, our social and cultural structures of feminine primacy have greased the wheels for an unconstrained natural narcissistic impulse to go unchecked. The ugly reality is that personality disorders including and going beyond those of narcissism destroy lives. Your narcissism and whatever personality disorders you are exhibiting and embracing are diminishing your life's potential for thriving in proportion to their derangement.

In part, this is understandable, as so much of our culture is influence by the radical 2nd wave of feminism, which embraced the politics of gender based narcissism where everything is about identity politics. Feminist revolutionaries were so clear to state, in Marxists terms, that "the personal is the political." They also were very clear about their objective to "destroy the patriarchy." Calling attention to and limiting feminine narcissism would only hamper those objectives of destroying the family. By fostering, supporting and enabling increasingly unconstrained feminine narcissism combined with hypergamy they were promoting those natural elements that would work against and destroy the family order. By supporting "pro-(promiscuous)-sex", "anti-slut", "pussy-hat" and "nasty woman", "man-spreading", "man-splaning" etc. campaigns, 3rd wave "social-justice warrior" feminists are once again showcasing a willingness to demonize men, masculinity, the family order and a willingness to sacrifice the masses, you and all the women who listen to this poison, to a philosophy that has only proven to lay waste to men, women and children alike, as good Marxists have always been willing to do.

The other component to cultural narcissism is that attention is the new cultural currency in the digital age and digital economy. Nowhere is this more acute than on social media platforms, which are fertile grounds for unabashed self-promotion, virtue signaling and attention validation absorption. It has also become fertile ground for identity politics where casual opinions and conversations have become incendiary calls for personal battle, where the art of character assassination and personal destruction are levied. Where the ever attempt to shift the conversation focus to yourself, your needs, your beliefs and how you've been victimized is omni present and a flowing personal narrative. In doing so, you've turned social manners inside out by the self-propagation of once personal and private accounts into public address. Couple that with a glass-like-vanity where you vocalize how "fierce" you are in waiting for the right man to recognize your worth, value and piety, that you're just not capturing the attention of and reaffirming it all through tear streaked eyes.

If I haven't said it before, you're patient zero of your life.

I'll provide one more as a Segway prior to going into our last example that women are facing in today's sexual marketplace: "the advice you take, is the advice you own."

As social, cultural and biological advice, feminism has wrought tremendous harm on men, women, children and to the great human institution of family. It further harms women and you in particular, because it is teaching good men, honorable men, men of virtue, to rationally lose their incentives to engage women in a crucial and essential manner and by increasing their risks in doing so. Men know what it is like to be on the unrelenting receiving end of negative social and cultural judgement based on their gender, but are not permitted, scorned, mocked and condemned as misogynists for speaking out and speaking up about their truths, injustices upon them and unfair diminishment. All of which is ultimately essential for their exploitation (a fish may not have need for a bicycle, but somehow it surely has need for that tax cash). When you embrace feminism and the tenants of feminism, you are broadcasting your unsuitability for commitment, for marriage, for motherhood. You are shunning the potential heroes of your life and love away; the men who are willing, able and capable of protecting, providing, and raising a family and legacy that will survive and thrive beyond both of you.

In today's SMP, women cannot play the "passive woman" script in the hopes that the love of their life will just simply come along, prepared, able and willing to take them away from the life they have constructed for themselves, nor from those who have drink heartily from a poisonous cup. If women want a relationship and a committed monogamous one, they are going to have to come to terms that they are both a consumer, as well as a service and product provider within the sexual marketplace and need to attend to themselves and their business accordingly to fulfill their lives and their life's objectives.

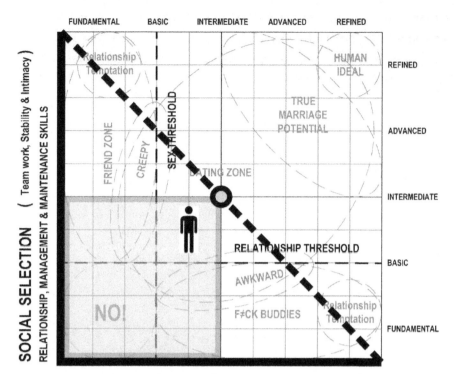

NATURAL SELECTION (Survival, Seduction & Provision)
PHYSICAL, SEXUAL & SOCIAL DISPLAY DIMORPHISMS

Dating Zone - Male Perspective

Before we analyze that actual map from a male perspective, it is important to remember men on a whole are expected and prompted biologically and culturally to seek and discriminate for a partner that arouses his interest sexually - Hypogamy. In meeting each of his biological requirements this means a downward projection of options from his overall SMP characteristic level. When people speak colloquially of being "out of his league" this reflects the common appreciation of these factors.

A man is unlikely to meet the "to protect" category from anyone and anything bigger, faster, meaner and fiercer than he is. That generally is a fact of nature. This holds true for us too. Furthermore, as a mating pair/couple/partnership goes, the male is

The MAP- A Personal Guide to the Sexual Marketplace

the disposable party biologically in nature; a mother has the ability to nurse and raise an infant alone, if required. As such, males on the whole, are expected to defend his family, to the extent that it may include the loss of his own life, so that they may live, and specifically his genetic material, his child, may survive. Because of this, his options are tended to be downward focused from his level of abilities to physically protect and safeguard.

With regards to his requirement to provide means he must actually produce. That is the nature of man. To produce. Not only produce, but to produce in abundance of his own needs and consumption. One cannot provide for others when one has no resources in excess of his own. Debt and diminishment are not a form of security or attraction based on hypergamy and hence not a viable option. Consequently, his mandate is to "over produce" to those he can provide to. Again, a downward projection from his SMP rating value.

The last criteria of raising a family is noted for his ability to maintain the previous two criteria over an extended period of time consistently, with increasing demands based on the increase of his family size and support structure, frequently encompassing additional and extended family members. Overall his ability to protect and to provide must consistently increase in ability to maintain stability and security overall. He has two general options here, initially be able to overproduce so that the family size may enlarge, or over produce in graduation with the size and level of his responsibilities. Again, a downward focus on SMP value.

> **Pro-Note:** ever notice the correlation between divorce rates and financial issues? In today's world, financial issues are akin to security and comfort issues of the old world. If a man is not able to keep up the security and comfort levels of his family, there is a known negative qualitative

experience here, but also a biological triggering of a woman's hypergamy that will drive her view point of the man, their relationship and her relationship with him.

In summation the three primary tenants of a man's life: to protect, to provide and to raise a family, in conjunction with a woman's hypergamy to marry up, all are inclined naturally to focus his attention for an appropriate mating prospect downward from his SMP value rating. Historically, culture has also reflected and promoted those inclination, as societies and groups don't fair well when failure is abundant and likely.

Because of all of that, graphically when we observe an average man's SMP value, we can conclude that he has remarkably small range of options from which he is likely to be successful in triggering a hypergamous feminine response. On a whole, an average man may command the attention of approximately the lowest 25% of the overall sexual marketplace. Furthermore 25% of his options are completely off limits as possibilities; both morally & legally, with a greater than 50% of his options are either below the Sex Threshold or the Relationship Threshold. That leaves a scant 16% of his option range as being within the rationally acceptable 'Dating Zone' range of options, yet all of his options are still below the relative 50% divorce threshold and all of his prospective partners have lower than average Natural or Social Selection traits (not good). For all that, a woman chosen from this range will hold an exclusive monopoly to his ability to provide and protect, but he must also surrender his biological hypogamous interests as well in this exchange. Therefore, given the average man, making an average partnering decision based on biological and cultural drivers, we can expect his life to be greatly diminished and at risk for significant failures. The limitation of abilities and traits of his prospective partners to command his interests, continued investment and to maintain their relationship are all factors that weigh against him.

We should also be reminded that while women tend to be the gate keepers of sex, men also tend to be the gate keepers for commitment. Simply put, _men must be compelled to commit_. He is the one who determines if there is a relationship or not. His choice to commit is his alone (outside of the utilization of force). The rise of second and third waves of feminism have done little to change these facts. With that in mind, a man still controls who he commits to and under what circumstances. To alleviate a great deal of self-induced misery brought on by the trauma of poor choices, men should invoke the "first do no harm" order of approach to whom he places his commitment to. To do so, a man must first know himself and secondly constrain himself from his base impulses and then choose wisely. We cannot ever remove risk completely froms any equation, but knowledge is the closest we can come to doing so.

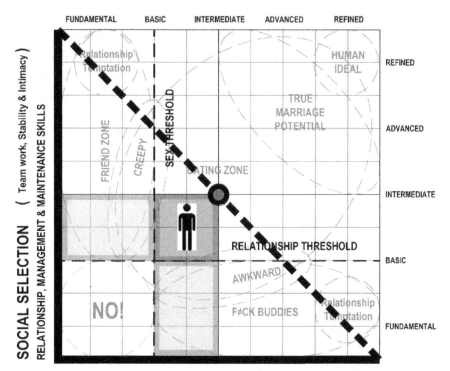

FUNDAMENTAL   BASIC   INTERMEDIATE   ADVANCED   REFINED

SOCIAL SELECTION (Team work, Stability & Intimacy)
RELATIONSHIP, MANAGEMENT & MAINTENANCE SKILLS

Relationship Temptation

HUMAN IDEAL   REFINED

TRUE MARRIAGE POTENTIAL   ADVANCED

FRIEND ZONE

CREEPY

SEX THRESHOLD

DATING ZONE   INTERMEDIATE

RELATIONSHIP THRESHOLD   BASIC

AWKWARD

NO!

F#CK BUDDIES

Relationship Temptation   FUNDAMENTAL

NATURAL SELECTION (Survival, Seduction & Provision)
PHYSICAL, SEXUAL & SOCIAL DISPLAY DIMORPHISMS

The Nature of Low Scoring SMP Women

When we consider the options for the average male in the SMP, just who are these potential prospects? What exactly are their character attributes and what are many of the unspoken implications of choosing a partner from within this group? As we have already pointed out, each of these individuals will be below average and trigger the risks associated with being average, only to a greater degree the further away from the mean they are. That is the risks are amplified as they have fewer positive traits and attributes to arouse our sexual interest, nor have the appropriate relationship skills to manage, maintain and sustain them. Let's take a closer look at the three quadrants of an average man's potential prospects and what it means to select someone from any of these ranges.

Below the Sex Threshold, but Above the Relationship Threshold

The first group, those below the sex threshold, doesn't arouse our hypogamy of sexual interest and therefore if we choose a partner here it is not out of our sex drive and desire, which is naturally the chemistry and glue which binds us together as a species (sex in sexual selection kind of being the most important). The driver of the choice will more than likely be from a sense of emotional damage we sustained earlier in life causing a high degree of lack of self-worth, self-esteem and fear of abandonment or failure. Not only that, but men who select in this range also had no support structure that would they would have benefited from greatly by teaching, enabling and developing those social behaviors that would have developed with knowledge, shared wisdom and experience to make better choices for themselves. But because of these earlier experiences, lack of mentoring and development, we feel unworthy, unlovable and incomplete, that we are simply not good enough to ask better for ourselves and fear the risks associated with additional rejection, betrayal or abandonment if we dare do so. Consequently, we choose a partner who is within our neglected means of expectations sexually. We normally see this in tremendously under-fathered men. Men who have been dominated by circumstances, inherent intra-male competition, projected female hypergamy standards and closely held associations with negative life experiences and have overly withdrawn as a result coupled with a "white knight" response to rescuing a victimized woman; commonly a projection of their own mother's fears, fragility, and insecurities (see single-mothers). Because of this he will tend to seek out a viable prospect within his means, that also has need for rescuing... the "ugly duckling of princeless Cinderellas."

Above the sex threshold, but below the Relationship Threshold

The second group, those above the sex threshold, will arouse our hypogamous interest sexually, but completely lacks the ability to connect or sustain intimacy beyond sex, or do so at below average ability (there's a reason for this). The concern here is that individuals who are unable to form social networks and lack intimacy skills naturally seek stimulus and drama to fill the void of intimacy. They may be exciting for a while, but it gets old fast. They ultimately tend to be high conflict individuals, abusive, persuasive blamers and victims who use the power and force of their emotions to sell their narratives by distortions, half-truths and lies. Women here will tend to be inexplicably narcistic, low-grade Machiavellian manipulators, yet strongly sociopathic (lacking empathy and conscious).

A classic example of this is when a conflict arises between utilizing appropriate means of behavior and inappropriate behaviors within their social networks, they will tend to always side with the most convenient and short-term advantageous choice of inappropriate behavioral choice. It is far easier to garner the short-term benefits and put off the long-term ramifications. Not only is it convenient, it is a pattern they are all too familiar and experienced with; a run to failure, over react, then either reconstitute (typically sexually to garner the greatest advantage and concessions) or replace the individual and begin anew. Simply wash, rinse and repeat with little to no personal introspection. There is a term for this self-absorbed, manipulative, drama queen; it's called crazy. There are two sure-fire ways to tell. The first is they have no problem telling you that they are crazy (but in that fun, cool way). The second way is to notice when they absolutely flip out when you imply that they are actually crazy. The ultimate problem with crazy isn't the fun and cool ride, but the fact that ultimately crazy won't be denied. Crazy got to do what crazy does and crazy won't take you, your feelings or interests into account.

So why do men continually fall prey to women in this category? Because sex is the primary driver for natural selection and the fact that this is mirrored culturally, it greatly amplifies and reinforces our limbic view that sex is the ultimate form of approval. This then becomes an obsessive pre-

The MAP- A Personal Guide to the Sexual Marketplace

occupation to meet that need, even at the expense of having our emotional and psychological needs left unfulfilled or terribly wanting. This lack of intimacy stabilization forms the bedrock of a dysfunction, to which our emphasis on sex as a surrogate for actual intimacy has squarely placed us.

With both of these categories the women are underdeveloped, socially, emotionally (lacking empathy and maturity), and sexually, who more than likely have tremendous voids in proper parenting, care, love, support and nurturing into being fully able and capable adults. Why do we know this? Because parented children thrive, and these women are not thriving. Furthermore, because we are mammals, we learn primarily, by impression through observation and direct experience. Her primary source for this impressions, most likely a single mother who makes poor choices, who couldn't keep, attract or maintain the interests of a good man around and fully exhibited the associated behaviors of relationship management you're likely going to be experiencing. As the saying goes, the apple doesn't fall far from the tree.

It is a sad and terrible statistic that single women coming from abusive relationships tend to choose a second partner who is (10X) more likely to physically abuse her child than her natural father. As a child she will be impressed by these experiences and relate them to men, and project them forward onto others. Worst of all are those that have been sexually abused, exploited and neglected. It is also a sad testament to human nature that, for survival sake the abused may bond with the abusers or those that have neglected them. They may minimize the abuse or justify it and the malevolent psychological process that generates a victim-to-victimizer cycle. Often this is by means of reacted defense psychology, where an abused victim preemptively strikes out at those whom she may feel threatened by (the imprinted skill sets). Worst of all are those individuals damaged at such a young age that it has affected their genetic brain development, in the form of being unable to establish empathy, or emotional connections with others.

When we consider these two groups on a whole in relation to the average male, what outcome can we envision as likely when we take notably under-developed adults, that are highly likely to be emotionally damaged, neglected and harmed and pair them with a male partner of average means? Life is difficult already. Life is harder when you're stupid about it. Life is incredibly difficult & miserable when you do both and add on adversity and hardship you are unprepared to handle it. And we haven't even discussed what individual health, pre-disposition to addictive substances, criminal history, in-laws, combined child households, financial debt, economic situation, livelihood/occupation, or regional social context adds to the mix, but we can probably bet safely it will involve several of if not more than these. If you haven't figured it out, and you're making these types of choices, you're going to find out. We also have term for this: Poverty. Not only financial poverty, but emotional, spiritual and moral poverty. A poverty of the human soul.

Above both Sex & Relationship Thresholds, but below average SMP

The last group, those above both the sex and relationship thresholds, will represent slightly reduced lunacy and improved incentives from both of the previous categories, but not much more beyond that. It really is a matter of degrees, as overall any woman below the normal of average, even if above minimal standards of acceptability, is still subpar in performance and benefits. And that is just out of the gate, we haven't even started to discuss the other disadvantages that are embedded with making a potentially life altering decision by choosing her. Even as your choices improve you're only nearing the break-even point of a 50% divorce threshold. Your life is a poor grade toss up, as you march to the grave...at best. In truth, it isn't even that. If you make a decision to choose a partner within this range, you evaluated yourself poorly, you aimed far too low, and still undershot your potential.

Another way of looking at this is if you really considered your relationship as a partnership. If you were hiring, what level are you hiring at? Someone within this range isn't a CEO, COO, or for that matter a chief of anything and won't be in your organization. They are not even Executive grade... No, you're not hiring a partner, officer or an executive, but rather an employee... the lower the SMP rating, the more likely they are an entry grade, minimum wage level of hire.

If you were dealt this hand in a Poker game, this isn't a hand you bluff with. It's a hand you fold on. The problem is that with a higher SMP score that starts to approach average, you're less, and less likely to fold. It's the close hands that draw us in and we're reluctant to let go of. This is the losing slowly strategy at gambling and life. We end up placing ourselves in a position not to win by thriving, but to work so hard at just maintaining, treading water and slowly and eventually losing anyway. It is far worse than if we had just initially just bet big, lost outright and then went on to recover from it.

Co-dependency & Oneitis

I realize that self-restraint and raising your standards for the people in your life will greatly limit your options, particularly if you remain average, but the higher you can retain standards of acceptability, the greater your life and life's rewards that will be attained. But that does mean getting comfortable with and remaining single. Unfortunately, for too many men, being alone is the equivalent of feeling lonely and this loneliness is an emotional burden that is too difficult to bear, as they cannot resist the psychological compunction that is found not only in sex, but the sense of acceptance and approval deriving from it. This psychological need formulates a basis of dependency and neediness for emotional and sexual validation. It forms the bulwark of a co-dependent relationship structure where they are giving, sacrificing and consumed with meeting the needs and desires of their partners. Often this "love" is motivated by emotional and psychological projection, not for the actual attributes and properties of their partner, but for what they represent; the filling of an earlier trauma and subsequent void left in their life, while activating the biological prompts that bind us together

The MAP- A Personal Guide to the Sexual Marketplace

sexually. Unfortunately, this combination of emotional, psychological need and sexual capitalization, is enough to form an addictive obsession to the relationship at hand, despite it's obvious flaws, failures and deficiencies. It concludes with a mental state colloquially knowns as "Oneitis", where the dependent does not know how to emotionally disconnect and let go of a failed relationship, despite harmful consequences to their mental health, personal, social and professional lives, particularly when their partner has already moved along and they have been disposed of unceremoniously. The immediate effects of neglect, rejection or abandonment of the current relationship, often resonates deeply held emotional trauma from the past, triggering an obsessive compulsion to behave toward the threatened, failing or failed relationship in a way that reinforces these insecurities overall.

Regrettably, this cycle will continue to play itself out, until the individual resolves the deeply seated emotional and psychological drivers of this underlying behavior. No amount of new sexual conquests or new relationships or other escape behaviors such as drugs, alcohol and violence will change the internal circumstances that are guiding and driving these choices and behaviors. Until you change, your story won't change. Wishing and wanting are not the same things as becoming aware of it, and doing the incredibly hard work to resolve it and have turned your wounds into wisdom.

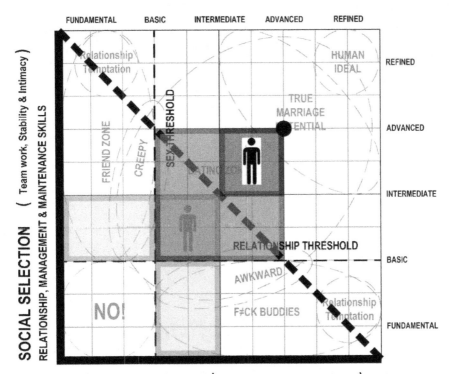

FUNDAMENTAL   BASIC   INTERMEDIATE   ADVANCED   REFINED

SOCIAL SELECTION (Team work, Stability & Intimacy)
RELATIONSHIP, MANAGEMENT & MAINTENANCE SKILLS

Relationship Temptation — HUMAN IDEAL — REFINED

SEX THRESHOLD — TRUE MARRIAGE POTENTIAL — ADVANCED

FRIEND ZONE — CREEPY — DATING ZONE — INTERMEDIATE

RELATIONSHIP THRESHOLD — BASIC

NO! — AWKWARD — F#CK BUDDIES — Relationship Temptation — FUNDAMENTAL

NATURAL SELECTION (Survival, Seduction & Provision)
PHYSICAL, SEXUAL & SOCIAL DISPLAY DIMORPHISMS

Male Competition- AMOG (Alpha Male Other Guy)

With all that being said, there is another important factor that our map showcases graphically, but is also relatively unspoken common knowledge, which is, our competitors are in fact our betters. That high SMP valued male, because of his high valued traits and attributes will not only out compete us but commands a greater range and spread of options that completely overlap your prime choice of potential prospects. As I noted in the female perspective, women within your prime prospect range will not only try to compete for his attention with similar high valued SMP females but will do so by undercutting them sexually to garner his attention-and will likely be successful in doing so. So not only are you competing with your better, but your prime prospects are incentivized by intra-sex female

The MAP- A Personal Guide to the Sexual Marketplace

competition to be aggressively sexual toward him and not you. This also means while she may be flirty, and attention whoring and requiring of your validation, she is also likely going to be resistant and potentially hostile toward any approach you may make, as she can ill afford to lose the fleeting attention of the alpha males within her grazing area or be seen as settling for average. That show she put on wasn't for you, you were just part of a greater audience to get his attention. The reality is she simply isn't there for average, when better is in supply.

Here's a little recap about the Alpha Male Other Guy:

- He's your better and will likely out compete you.
- The prime female prospects in your range will compete sexually for him, but not you.
- She will be defensive and resisting of your approach because you are not her prime prospect.
- She's looking for better than "average", which isn't you.

There's no getting around it, this sucks! It also explains the increase in difficultly associated with self-improvement beyond average. You have your own inertia to get past, the mass of the actual work involved, and the resistance associated with any movement through this arena associated with others, let alone the added weight of errors of knowledge and judgement you're carrying with you, which honestly is the first thing you should let go of if you want to improve.

Unforced Errors

Because of the factors and dynamics implied with the AMOG, average guys tend to make a series of unforced errors: mistakes of reasoning and errors of judgement that result in missed opportunities and blunders that are entirely self-induced. Whether the AMOG realizes or knows this is irrelevant, but it does create added leeway for him to be more successful than you.

The MAP- A Personal Guide to the Sexual Marketplace

Overt Attention, Validation and Approval

The first unforced error is to provide attention, validation and approval to women who are attractive and within your general presence, particularly if they are generating an overall show. This is a tell, a signal that belies your SMP position, as being truly an "average" dude and this "show" isn't something you are familiar with or common for you. Actual AMOGs are accustomed to lower value women flaunting themselves to garner attention of the AMOG, as a result he is going to have differing expressions of reactions to this behavior. Again, she isn't looking for average, and when you provide overt signals of interest, need and desire, she will lose whatever interest you may have legitimately garnered, because she hasn't earned your attention or signaled its desirability. The AMOG on the other hand may acknowledge her and her display behaviors to elicit increased or sustained levels of display behaviors to increase the overall sexual atmosphere and to ramp up intra-female competition, but not those behaviors associated with a desire to actual close the deal sexually with her. It's an approval of the sexuality display and competition displays for his attention, not the actual girl.

Undercutting Sexual Enticement with Commitment

The second unforced error average guys do is that when they do elicit attention and receptivity from women, they attempt to spike their value by undercutting and proffering what the AMOG seemingly withholds from these women; commitment. And that's a deal killer here. Here's a direct comparison: when a lower value woman undercuts her betters by offering sex, what is the term generally utilized to describe her? "Slut." While she may actually get the AMOG to sleep with her, he won't commit to her. She just "Fuck Buddied" herself. Same is true with the average guy, but in reverse. In too easily offering up or providing commitment to negotiate a sexual deal, you've lost your end result. She'll take the commitment, like the AMOG does the sex, but won't be providing the sex, just as he doesn't provide the commitment. You've just friend zoned yourself. Average guys keep doing so, endlessly chasing and chasing willing to repeat and double down on their previous errors of committing too soon and without reciprocity, to no avail. This is a form of oversharing. When one party provides too much, too fast that hasn't been mutually developed in reciprocated forms of expression.

Folding in the Face of Adversity

A significant forced error that the average/common guy either senses intuitively or has enough adverse experience regarding is to simply fold in the face of all this adversity. To give in. To quit and lower his sights and options down below the level that an AMOG, or perceived AMOG may provide interest to, to limit the overall competition level. Left to our own devices, we are habitually our worst critic and naysayer. Without a close friend or support group to offer a countering position we are only left with the negative thoughts and experiences in our heads, which will shape how we view ourselves and the possibilities of the world before us. The reality is, if most "average" SMP guys understood and practiced not making forced errors and just brushed up on a little game (fun, social, sexual enticement, provocation and play) it would shift their rating for the better and they would close the distance on the AMOG and his perceived sexual monopolization of the SMP. When you combine that with a support group that would encourage positive behavioral patterns and be there to support and nurture you through both successes and failure, but keeping the failures objectively figured, it is a tremendous advantage over the average man who doesn't have it. In fact, I would argue that most 'average' guys who do, are above average because of this social network and the benefits derived from it.

The Static SMP

A follow up on this is the assumption that the SMP is static. That the AMOG, always has the upper hand. That context, or the situation and

The MAP- A Personal Guide to the Sexual Marketplace

dynamics of a micro SMP don't apply, but in fact they do. In an earlier chapter I mention micro-utilization of the SMP Map based on immediate situational context. Average guys don't understand or utilize this and too willfully bleed value, when they could hold onto it to capitalize on later. How often does an AMOG Fuck up and lower his SMP value by doing something stupid, overly aggressive or dominant that is off putting to women? More than they would care to admit. That is a life opening, if you're prepared and willing to take it, but it will require assertiveness and aggressiveness to do so, which is a hypergamous attraction and arousal trigger which women are biologically inclined for. Remember, behaviors drive perception. Change your behaviors, change her perception.

Arousal Transference

Understand that the AMOG is also trying to seal the best deal he can obtain, just as women are. It is common for an AMOG to elicit value and female competition by distributing his attention around and among female groups (pro note: this is the value of being openly social). The girls in your prospect range may get some of that attention, but she may not be able to hold onto it or is not the actual target for his attention. Subsequently, another one of life's openings just occurred. A key biological reality is knowing that once sexual arousal is initiated, it tends to simmer, not go immediately cold. No one likes to get hot and bothered and then doused with ice water. Because of this sexual transference is the norm. Same is true sexually, particularly when emotional validation is also at stake and many Pick Up Artists have noted that a woman's "buying temperature" is transferrable. That is, her arousal may have been initiated by an individual (AMOG), an environment (club) or occasion (bridal parties, weddings and funerals are notorious for this) and that it is transferable to whomsoever she chooses to direct it toward. Which is why so many people are inclined to go to environments that proffer stimulating, voyeuristic and arousing venues for socialization (club scene). It promotes sexualized behavior, and feeds choices that we would not do cold without this environmental prompting.   (Pro Note: trying to combine all three or more for added effect).

Valuing Game

A big differentiator between an AMOG and an average guy is that the AMOG understands his marketing, sales and he is able to close the deal. This is one of the areas of Hypergamy that most average guys don't get, are too afraid to implement on a regular basis and are uncertain as a result when it counts. Hypergamy includes deliberate sexual enticement, provocation and execution. In essence, all the social sexual tenants of game. These are skills. They can be taught. They can be learned. They can be honed, and they can be developed. The question an average guy should be asking himself is not if he should learn game, it's "is getting her worth learning game?"   The answer is "yes" and beyond that, biologically, her Hypergamy demands it. Until he does, she isn't going to be as intrigued, interested or aroused. In fact, until he does, he's missing out on not only 1/3 of her Hypergamous nature, but the actual heart of sexual interest and selection.

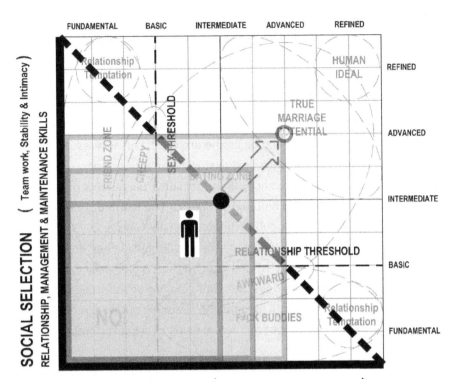

FUNDAMENTAL   BASIC   INTERMEDIATE   ADVANCED   REFINED

SOCIAL SELECTION (Team work, Stability & Intimacy)
RELATIONSHIP, MANAGEMENT & MAINTENANCE SKILLS

REFINED
ADVANCED
INTERMEDIATE
BASIC
FUNDAMENTAL

Relationship Temptation

HUMAN IDEAL

TRUE MARRIAGE POTENTIAL

FRIEND ZONE

CREEPY

SEX THRESHOLD

RELATIONSHIP THRESHOLD

AWKWARD

NO!

F*CK BUDDIES

Relationship Temptation

NATURAL SELECTION (Survival, Seduction & Provision)
PHYSICAL, SEXUAL & SOCIAL DISPLAY DIMORPHISMS

Self-Improvement Incentivization

The most reassuring observation to be made from the SMP Map is that
males are incredibly incentivized to improve their characteristics and traits
within the sexual marketplace through self-restraint and self-improvement,
particularly when Natural Selection traits are paired with Social Selection
traits. In doing so, their option range increases significantly in comparison
to their efforts associated with personal gain, unlike women, who see the
inverse. It is here that learning, developing and gaining confidence within
the realms of social and sexual dynamics starts to pay off handsomely and
are relatively cost effectively, as we are not talking about a massive shift
from one end of the spectrum to the other, but a graduated shift from mid-

intermediate skill level to mid-advance level. It's just a natural progression in your knowledge, awareness and abilities, in fact your development as a man.

The other factor to consider isn't just the increase in the qualitative nature of your life. By having prospects who actually represent an ability to secure, nurture and support a relationship appropriately, you have the very direct option to exclude those that don't. As we saw in the *Average* section, by moving positively away from average one reaps the rewards of being certain and in control, while also removing much of the risks associated with being uncertain and out of control. All of these contribute to a vastly overall reduced risk throughout many of life's spectrums, one of which is a rapid departure from the average divorce threshold.

As a man, you are not only the architect of your own life, but the relationships and relationship structures you choose to create for yourself. In this regard, I'm reminded of the fable of the Three Little Pigs, who each go out and build their own houses to live in. Don't build your life around the wishful thinking of straw and being average.

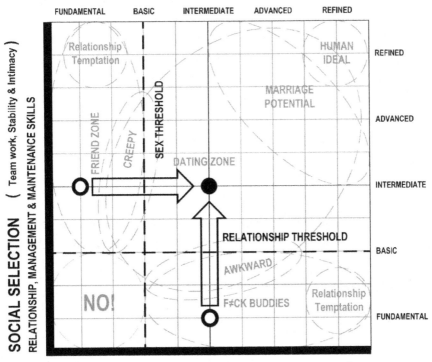

NATURAL SELECTION (Survival, Seduction & Provision)
PHYSICAL, SEXUAL & SOCIAL DISPLAY DIMORPHISMS

The Start of any Monumental Journey

Self-discovery, self-improvement and life reconstruction is an art form. One grounded in your narrative of your past, your self-regard and beliefs of what's possible. It is foremost a personal journey with more than a thousand steps, trials and tribulations that you will feel acutely. Everyday this journey begins anew, every hour, and every moment lived. As every experience shifts into the past, with tomorrows promises arriving today and lived in the present now. These daily, hourly, moment-to-moment journeys begin internally, with your thoughts, both conscious and unconscious. It is here that all of our journeys will start, and because of that it is here that we need to prepare initially. We need to prepare ourselves mentally and emotionally to step out of the ordinary and into the reality of who we want to become and project that ideal forward in the behaviors and traits that we will personify, often in defiance of our past and current sense of belief.

I believe these journeys need to and should start off with empathy, kindness and fairness to yourself, not beratement and belittlement. Too much of our future is weighed down by the awareness of our past, constrained in our sense of beliefs and manifested in acceptance of those limitations. We need to make peace with our past to move beyond it. Otherwise we will carry the weight of that past well beyond its usefulness. This will means coming to peace with who you were, your life, its form, your relationships with others and all the failures and grievances, both real and imagined, but we must not remain here. Resolve that which needs to be resolved. Let go of what needs to be let go of, and then turn away from the past and look toward the future. The past will remain whether or not we stare at it, and the future will arrive whether or not we are prepared or even witness its coming. The past doesn't demand that it be relived, but only remembered.

It is one thing to hold up an ideal, a destination or goal, but it is another to project yourself having already obtained and living in that state already, naturally. Your future self-achieved. Your future realized, not in ideal abstract, but in an already existing form able to be a constant companion to guide and support your current self. We knowingly hear the voices in our heads of our past, why not the voices of our future? Of our potential achieved? Why not have a countenance to internalized emotional objections that always come up? Self-improvement by its nature and definition mean self-actuated. Inherent in this is also mentoring. Why rely on the flawed you, the insecure you, the one that's below your potential? Why not the you fully realized and actualized? Think of what today's you would tell the past you. We'd have a lot to say and with sound advice. What do you think your imagined future you would express for you now, if it was able? Undoubtedly the future you would show more compassion and empathy for who you are today but coupled with the knowledge and support for you to desperately achieve what you have already achieved. In the taking of your journey, having this companion at your side to guide your thoughts and choices is invaluable. The notion of 'What would my future-self do, my better-self do, the person I want to become?' is an outstanding beacon to travel by. It will also give you solace in the various failures and setbacks that we will all sustain, in knowing that the overall doing is more important than the immediate outcome.

Understanding the Basics

Undertaking a journey of self-improvement to the degree which we've been discussing is recognizing then coming to terms with the realization that we are committing ourselves to a vow of improvement, not idealization and perfection. It is a dedication to the betterment of you today than you were in the past and projecting those lessons learned into your behaviors, beliefs and attitudes for tomorrow. It is also the acknowledgement that our ambitions for tomorrow exceed our abilities of today. There should be fear and natural emotional trepidation, but those fears should be turned into courage and inspiration which are found and acted upon. With all this should emerge additional inspiration to challenge and to beckon us forward. When we act in this regard, we are living and acting virtuously. When we behave virtuously we enlarge ourselves, we embolden ourselves, we grow, we thrive and we shine. We truly live and the result of that is we find happiness as a consequence. When we don't act and behave virtuously, when we exhibit vice, we diminish ourselves, our lives and we rob ourselves of what could have been; greatness. And we know it. And we can never hide that fact from ourselves. We have to live with the knowledge that we could have, should have, but didn't choose better. Ultimately our lives are a reflection of that.

Recognizing the Obstacles

For each of us, the vastness and certainty of what lies before us can develop into anxiety and extreme apprehension at the scale and magnitude of what we aspire to and what that aspiration commands in response to meet it. It is normal to feel a whelming up of insecurities and apprehension when facing this. The key is to listen to those fears, apprehensions and worries and then determine if they are legitimate or not. If they're not legitimate, neither is your worrying about them. So stop it. When you worry needlessly you're self-soothing for failure. That's not what we want and isn't of benefit. If your worries and anxieties are legitimate the question to face is can you control them or are they out of your control? If they are out of your control, leave worrying about fate to the gods. (There is a degree of satisfaction in delegating to the gods... as if you're saying "you handle this") Now, when we've identified those worries and anxieties that are legitimate and within our control, what are they and what do we know about them? This is where planning, preparation and conditioning (experience) is crucial to overcoming them and your anxieties surrounding them. These are things we can learn in advance, to avoid or minimize the adverse results. What was previously or would have been a crisis turns into an inconvenience that we can manage when planned for in advanced.

Have Patience

Nobody being vulnerable to a process that is new, challenging and audacious can avoid holding in the back of their head thoughts that failure is a probability. We know it is. In many ways we prepare ourselves for that. We go through a series of failure soothing processes to lessen and make the acceptance of failure more accommodating. But what we do not take into account is the very real probability that when we apply ourselves and lean into the changes we accepted and committed to, that we will not see the results we want or expected in comparison to others. Are we prepared to deal with the lack of results, as a known obstacle and variable on our change journey? Popular culture too often lays claim that this will only happen inches from our goal, but the reality is that this inertia of results is endemic throughout the entire process and journey. The entire thing. If we are going to pursue this matter, we will need to address the matter appropriately. Is it truly a failure of results? Or is it that we expect too much too fast and smaller variables that we are not tracking, aware of or have dismissed, are playing a cumulative role in our lack of advancement? In moments such as this, it is good to slowly and carefully take stock. To relax and not emotionalize the issue, and then to circle back onto the facts as we know them, look for extraneous elements that may be factoring in and observe. Is what we are feeling true? Done right this will take time. . This is called patience. It's a wonderfully hard-won skill, and like all skills it is difficult until it is made easy by repetition, practice and experience.

Have Persistence

Patience alone isn't always going to resolve the issue of a lack of result. We have to persevere in our persistence of our goal. We need to recommit to ourselves, our goals and our vision regularly lest it escape us. We need to seek out and recognize that every gain is a gain, however small. Even if the gain is the acknowledgement of applying patience and persistence in the face of inertia. Realizing that we have likely overestimated the timetable, level of results, overfed ourselves with the anticipated desired results and are emotionally reacting to all of this, don't become inflexible and defeated. Instead view these moments as expected challenges, to which you are prepared to further commit and respond appropriately to, instead of wildly against. It is here the willingness to persist while measured in scale of inches that becomes monumental in the achievement of your goals and vision, because inertia didn't become a set-back that then culminated in failure. Ask yourself a question, "How would your expectations and emotional understanding change if you cared deeply for long term results?" A follow up to this is "if process and journey took twice as long to achieve your objective, would it still be worth it?"

Apply Perspiration

Ultimately when everything is all said and done, you simply have to do the work. There is no substitute for the perspiration of application. Action is the kinetic energy of achievement. We need to harness the pattern of action in order to achieve. We have to move off of center, away from our comfort zone, change the way we have been doing things to achieve the results we haven't been getting. I have never met nor heard of (nor do I expect to) anyone who's meaningfully achieved that didn't put in a tremendous amount of work. They were all work horses. Across the board they have all said that the work pays for itself. It pays better when you do it smartly. When you know what you are doing. When you know why you are doing it. But there is no escaping the requirement for work. Of putting the effort in and in quantities that would lead to success.

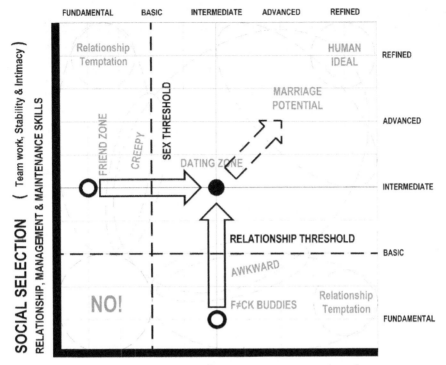

FUNDAMENTAL   BASIC   INTERMEDIATE   ADVANCED   REFINED

SOCIAL SELECTION (Team work, Stability & Intimacy)
RELATIONSHIP, MANAGEMENT & MAINTENANCE SKILLS

Relationship Temptation

HUMAN IDEAL — REFINED

MARRIAGE POTENTIAL

— ADVANCED

FRIEND ZONE

CREEPY

SEX THRESHOLD

DATING ZONE

— INTERMEDIATE

RELATIONSHIP THRESHOLD

— — — — — — — — — BASIC

AWKWARD

NO!

F#CK BUDDIES   Relationship Temptation

— FUNDAMENTAL

NATURAL SELECTION (Survival, Seduction & Provision)
PHYSICAL, SEXUAL & SOCIAL DISPLAY DIMORPHISMS

Average is a Terminal Disease

Take a look at the bigger picture of yourself and your life. Get clear on how your current personal culture (how your deeply held values and beliefs are behaviorally expressed) and how those are contributing to or hindering your success. How does it have a greater effect on who you are, where you are at, and what opportunities lay before you than the external forces arrayed against you? Your mindset is how you interact with the world...but firstly how you inner-react with yourself. This is something you control, but likely don't have command over. It is a form of control or lack thereof that is shaping your life greater than anything around you. So not only do you actually have the opportunity to control a great deal of your world, by having command of yourself, but you have the obligation to do so. Your mind and the cubic foot of space your physical brain commands is the most valuable volume of real estate you will ever own. To capitalize on it and to get it to work for you, you are going to have to rehabilitate your ambition. To rekindle and re-establish your fire within.

A good first step in this regard is to reject complacency and mediocre standards of behaviors. To treat your acceptance of "average" as a terminal disease. In the previous chapter on the nature of average I discussed how "average" isn't certain. It isn't in control. It isn't managed. That these states are highly unattractive. That "average" is at risk because of its mediocre nature. That "average" doesn't attract nor drive investment in it. There's little value in "average" and it is particularly diminished when easily compared to extraordinary. Why continue to live there?

Average doesn't seek to improve. Above average does. Above asks "what can I do today to improve my success?" It recommits daily, hour to hour, moment to moment to their purpose, vision and goals. They focus on the future and solutions to achieving it, with minimal but appropriate regard to the past. They do not attend board meetings in their own head where they berate, chastise and lay blame, fault and error with themselves endlessly. Instead they channel their thoughts toward improving, responding to resulting feedback and finding improved solutions to the challenges they face.

Acquiring a "spirit" to succeed requires being above average, which truly means having an open acceptance of the hardships, pain and failures along the way. And responding to those without being defined by them. It is about achieving clarity where utter commitment is placed. It is about finding the power of earned momentum that comes with an organized, committed and sustained effort. But it will never happen if you don't feel you deserve it, are worthy of the rewards, or are capable of the effort.

This is why when you put in the time and energy and effort to improve things, you are signaling to yourself and those around you that you are a master of your own future and destiny. You can see and experience the small results and wins first hand, immediately. Take pride is these steps and wins. Recognize that they are indeed personal signals to of your commitment. In time, these internalized signals will start to resonate outward and you will begin to project these signals. It's what's referred to as cognitive resonance. When you hold yourself in regard for having meaningful achievement, others will pick up on this and treat you with the same regard for which you hold yourself.

Mediocrity and complacency may be the default human nature, but we don't have to succumb to it. Our mindsets are malleable, and we have the ability to influence and control our own minds. When we succumb to average or our mediocre nature we let go of our sense of agency, purpose and investment into the underlying elements of our success and we live proportionally diminished lives.

Remove the negatives first

As we transition in our self-improvement journey from planning and mindset, our first order of business will be focused on those elements that will offer *the greatest rewards for the least amount of effort*. In effect we are going to go about picking the low hanging fruits of opportunity while they are ripe and succulent. Unfortunately, most people assume that the "improvement" in self-improvements means increasing or adding a skill or complexity into the existing equation. The truth couldn't be further from that. Just as with mindset, where a negative mindset will get in the way of success and opportunity, holding onto negative behavioral traits or permitting a noticeably deficient personality trait or expression to continue to manifest itself will not only pose a frictional cost, but telegraph in alarming ways and volume an incongruency within your make up. As an animal species we are hard-wired to pay attention to these as these were indicators of threats and dangers. It is because of this that the human psyche places a disproportionate analysis weight on negative conditions. In fact, we don't place a weighted disproportionate response to it, but an overly disproportionate response to it, to the effect of a 400% to a positive to break even. To turn a negative experience into a positive one has indicated an 800% response value. That is for every single negative it takes at least four positive experiences to neutralize the negative. And that's for an "ugh" response. To overlook a negative experience, you'll need at least eight positive experiences. Take a look at your own life and emotionally recall how you felt about a negative experience. How many positive experiences would YOU need to reverse that?

Not only is removing a negative trait or behavior far more beneficial and effective, it's simpler to accomplish. It won't be easy. Nothing worth doing generally is, but the harder the challenge is to accomplish, the greater the reward for having accomplished it.   All of the negative traits and behaviors we are exhibiting we are also in control of. You have command of them. You are not reliant on anyone or anything else to effect positive change in doing so. Unlike mastering a new skill or ability, it does not require achieving the successful navigation of several new steps in sequence to achieve the desired result. You just need to interrupt the pattern of behavior that leads to the expression of the negative trait or behavior in the first place. This will require knowledge and awareness of the elements at issue, coupled with self-control and discipline to limit the negative impact you're introducing into the equation.

Focus on a Fundamental
It is said the having a mastery of fundamentals is senior to change. That change, despite a mastery of fundamentals is an error because the impetus for change usually is a result of a fundamental deficiency or failure and subsequent modifications will not correct that underlying issue. Based on this, there should be a sincere self-examination of your understanding and mastery of the fundamentals.

For the basis of the Map of the Sexual Marketplace I utilize two primary drivers, Natural Selection and Social Selection, as prime axes that form the X and Y of our map. Within each of those drivers I broke out a series of three primary traits that compose those:

Natural Selection:

Physical display dimorphisms
Sexual display dimorphisms
Social display dimorphisms

Social Selection:
Relationship skills
Relationship management
Relationship maintenance

To understand your positioning within the sexual marketplace you were to analyze your abilities and traits in each category, combine the selection category (Natural & Social) into an average that then represented a two-digit grid coordinate. For this exercise, we are NOT going to combine the selection categories into an average but let them stand on their own. Which of these is the lowest? That trait will likely support the greatest advantage to improvement for the least amount of effort. Why? Because a basic trait is easier and more efficiently improved over an advanced or refined trait or skill. Not only that, but an unchecked deficiency that is disproportionate from your other attributes will resonate an incongruency that will set off alarm bells. However, you may be in need of a tie-breaker between selection traits. In this case, always default toward Natural Selection traits. We're sexual animals and our secondary purpose beyond survival is species replication. If, however you need a tie-breaker within a selection trait, I would favor improving that trait in which you feel less inclined to commit to. That measure of resistance is an emotional indicator of a greater weakness. Remember I'm not advising you to feel more comfortable, or indulge in complacency, but to improve.

Now that the trait and attribute has been identified you are going to have to do a measure of research and development to better understand these - self educate. In that regard, you are going to have the worst teacher in the world; yourself. Really. Most of your efforts are going to be self-directed, self-researched and self-documented, but you're in luck. There's a whole world of resources out there on the World Wide Web. Unfortunately, you're going to have to also make heads and tails of it all. Discover who's good verses who's well-meaning or clueless. Keep in mind that once you accept and take advice, you and you alone own the consequences. So, keep a keen eye out and cross reference content for veracity.

The MAP- A Personal Guide to the Sexual Marketplace

Exercise the Fundamental

If change had a basic sequence of awareness + knowledge + action, this last step, "action" is the scariest and emotionally the most challenging. Awareness may strike us like a slap in the face, but deep down I think we realize that it is better to be slapped with the truth than to continue to be kissed with a lie. Unfortunately, we can also delude ourselves in the revelation of knowledge, particularly new-found knowledge and assume that this alone will affect change. Regrettably it will not. Life isn't like that. Life requires experience and that is the combined effect of knowledge, coupled with action and unforeseen conditions and responses we could hardly anticipate. It is here, in the school of hard knocks that we really learn. When we apply ourselves, our awareness and understanding that come under test and review. Life will let you know where you stand, one way or another.

It is for these reasons that I recommend that you develop an exercise plan where you systematically develop and exercise those particular traits and attributes you're focusing on. Like any development of skill and ability, utilize the "crawl, walk, run" build up. It is far better to go slow and methodically, than to get carried away with unmeasurable efforts. The issue here is while the attempt may be in the right vein, the application may be miss-directed or applied resulting in a failure and a developed lack of confidence in the process. You don't teach people to learn to swim by throwing them in the deep end of the pool. This is traumatizing, not training. Your goal is to develop a training program that you can execute on and repeat over a period of time, to get a broad spectrum of results and feed back to properly assess improvements and deficiencies. This is a form of beta testing skills and abilities, rather than a product.

While short-range programs are enticing because of the immediacy of the promised results, they seldom work or are sustainable. It is far better to look 90-days out and chart a pattern course over that period to have adequate assessment and refinement before you can be sure the results are genuine and that you'll remain compliant.

Envisioning and Enacting Goals

The MAP- A Personal Guide to the Sexual Marketplace

Envisioning should be the guiding force behind our actions. Our goals should be large enough that they create a sense of inspiration and trepidation surrounding them, otherwise they will be of little value or merit in proportion to the effort to achieve them. We should examine our lives from point to point and ask ourselves, "What truth am I denying?" "What truth will strike me to the bone?" Those truths will be consequential. A shallow truth will ring hollow. It is these deep truths that we are ignoring that we truly need to address before it becomes too late or the consequences are too dire.

 To affect change, takes about 90-days of concentrated work and effort. To have those changes integrated into our lives and character will take considerably longer. It is natural to have goals set up for a convenient timeline, and none is more popular than a yearly resolution. The problem with a yearly defined goal isn't that change can't happen in that time, it's just typically we underestimate our ability to achieve it within that time frame. Conversely, we also tend to underestimate a four or five-year goal. In that regard it is far better to have and hold grander ideals of a five-year plan and hold yourself accountable than it is to have a series on individual one-year resolutions.

The most effective goal planning is one that takes the five-year envisioning and breaks the process down into yearly progression steps, and then again from yearly to quarterly and monthly. Remember what gets written down, gets accomplished. Personally, I have even broken my individual goal tasking into weekly assignments that I can keep track of and help monitor myself with achieving. I usually do this on a word document, with each page dedicated to a specific time-frame bench mark that is typically subcategorized by individual subject matter.

While all this sounds nice and good, what I've so far described is nothing but a tremendous to-do task list... Nobody likes this. I know I didn't. To the point I resented reviewing it each time I opened it and it became a

The MAP- A Personal Guide to the Sexual Marketplace

hinderance even thinking about it. The solution to this for me was to create an individual page for my personal "wins". Those tasks that showed up on the list that got accomplished we then moved to the "win" or "accomplished" page for that year. Each time I opened up the file, I made myself review the "wins" prior to closing, to see and remember each and every one of them. This was an acknowledgment of achieved success. It developed momentum the more I won. In fact, each year when I start over, I'm anxious to place wins immediately. Same for the end of year, where I want to stack that year's successes. It may sound crazy, but for me it worked.

The other thing that I did previously in my life, particularly where I was looking to affect change was journaling. This was instrumental for not only releasing and expressing pent up energy into something usable but was critical in several ways to observe those conditions that lead up to a failure or deficiency in performance. Other times, I would go back and realize that I strayed from my goals and progression because I had failed to incorporate something appropriately that I accurately identified earlier. Life gets in the way at times and we forget where we were. Having a written document, literally notes to yourself, proved crucial for me.

The last item I have utilized over the course of my life and have never regretted is champagne. Life in our times can be celebrated. If we are not prepared or in a habit of celebrating life's little victories, we will be highly unlikely and accustomed to celebrating the major victories. As a signal and in preparation of my successes and reward I've always kept a bottle of champagne in my refrigerator. At times in my life there was little to keep that bottle company, but I still always managed a split of champagne (tiny bottle meant for two). It was a daily reminder. I knew it was there. It was patient. It awaited my success, even when I was impatient. Furthermore, it was a critical declaration at the height of some of my personal failures, that despite the loss I was determined to try again. And so yes, after several personal catastrophes, I opened a bottle and vowed to try again. Over the years, those occasions became rarer and rarer as I suspect they will with you too.

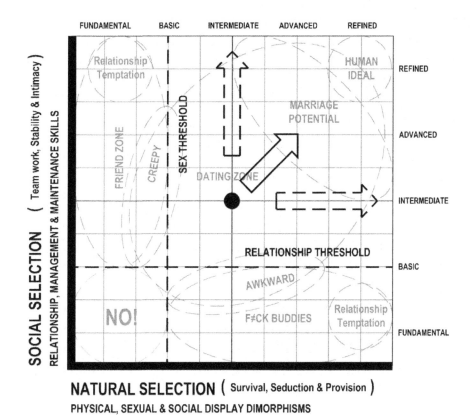

FUNDAMENTAL   BASIC   INTERMEDIATE   ADVANCED   REFINED

SOCIAL SELECTION (Team work, Stability & Intimacy)

RELATIONSHIP, MANAGEMENT & MAINTENANCE SKILLS

Relationship Temptation

FRIEND ZONE

CREEPY

SEX THRESHOLD

DATING ZONE

HUMAN IDEAL — REFINED

MARRIAGE POTENTIAL — ADVANCED

INTERMEDIATE

RELATIONSHIP THRESHOLD — BASIC

AWKWARD

NO!

F#CK BUDDIES

Relationship Temptation — FUNDAMENTAL

NATURAL SELECTION (Survival, Seduction & Provision)

PHYSICAL, SEXUAL & SOCIAL DISPLAY DIMORPHISMS

Choosing an Appropriate Path

The majority of the work that I have done within the dating community has been with individuals within the Friend or Fuck Buddy Zones or who were "average" but were not grounded with their understanding of the sexual marketplace, their position in it, or why their boat wasn't floating. They all tended to find my work either calling them to the middle or helping them to orientate themselves within the middle ground. While this book was written to help address each of their concerns and to do so in ways that were specific to them (identifying their deficiencies and appropriate response strategies), it isn't necessary to actually do the calculating defined within this book and get hyper specific as to what and how to proceed. Furthermore, for most people who become comfortable and happy with

The MAP- A Personal Guide to the Sexual Marketplace

being average, you really don't have a need or a desire to make this part central in their life... they want to get past a generalized pain point and move on. So, with that in mind, I offer a less detailed and more intuitive approach to orientating from average and going from there.

Before we dive in, a few questions first to set the tone and table for the discuss that will follow: Who are you? Where are you at in your life trajectory? And what will be your defining life story; comedy or tragedy? How are you playing that out?

To be fair and to help place our judgement within an honest and legitimate context for analysis, how do we evaluate this? To what standards should we hold ourselves to and in particular to our pursuit of human virtues?

The Aristotelian view of virtue is the zone and appropriate point between a gross deficiency and manifest excess of a trait. The appropriate point is not the mathematical middle or mean, but what he defined as a "golden mean"; that point which resides "at the right times, about the right things, toward the right people, for the right end and in the right way." Context is as important to content. It is developing the knowledge, self-awareness and wisdom to know what to do and then exhibiting the virtue of doing it and getting it done. The art is in the personal and unique style, wit and expression in which the actions and results are achieved. We ultimately thrive when we grow well, to do well.

With that in mind, I would guide any individual who is looking to improve their lives to simply "Go West!"

"Go West!"

For individuals either in the Friend or Fuck Buddy Zone, it doesn't take a genius to point you in the direction of "Average" and tell you to start walking. Getting hung up on bullshit won't serve you or your cause. To get to a better place than where you're at, you're going to have to pick up, move and relocate yourself. You are going to have to change. Sorry, but remaining the same self you currently are will only lead to a continuation of current results.

Heading to "average" or "Going West" doesn't have to be a specific spot and it clearly doesn't have defining features of place or arrival to signal when you've arrived. It's a lot like Kansas, tremendously immense with a richness and opportunity that didn't exist from where you came.

As I mentioned previously, average can seem like a warm and welcoming place. It just depends upon what we compare it to and the perspective of how we observe it. If you want to grow roots here, raise a family, grow old and pass away into dust here, fine. Truly! But if your goal and ambition was not to settle in Kansas/average but was really California/marriage potential and your wagon wheels broke or fell off on the way, my suggestion is to winter here. Then fix that shit and keep moving West.

Do you really need to know what part of California you want to head to? No. Just head West. That is, you just have to have a dedication to becoming better than average on a regular basis and you're going to end up there, one step at a time. If you lean overly heavy in one direction of Social Selection or Natural Selection you're still going to wind up in either Northern or Southern California, but it will still be California. You can tailor these concepts as fine or as loose as you like, but just **"Go West!"**.

Made in the USA
Columbia, SC
26 October 2018